AVIATION IN NORTH CAROLINA

A HISTORY

MICHAEL C. HARDY

Published by The History Press
An imprint of Arcadia Publishing
Charleston, SC
www.historypress.com

Front cover: (*Upper left*) Lieutenant Philippe H.X. de Gaulle (*right*) receives instruction at the U.S. Navy preflight training program at the University of North Carolina at Chapel Hill. *United States Navy*. (*Right*) The Wright Brothers National Memorial has a full-size replica of the *Wright Flyer* in bronze. *Author's collection*. (*Bottom left*) WASP head toward their airplanes at Camp Davis. *Texas Women's University*.
Back cover: Victor Borge and his orchestra visited North Carolina in late 1945. *Author's collection*.

First published 2025

Manufactured in the United States

ISBN 9781467156417

Library of Congress Control Number: 2024952009

CONTENTS

Preface 5

1. Before the Wright Brothers:
Early Aviation in North Carolina 7

2. Twelve Seconds at Kitty Hawk 12

3. Barnstorming and Aerial Combat:
1909–1918 22

4. Lindbergh, Rickenbacker and Earhart:
The Golden Age of Aviation 35

5. Watching the Skies and Protecting the Coast:
Aviation in North Carolina During World War II 68

6. "You Can Get There from Here":
Post–World War II Commercial Aviation and the Cold War 104

7. A Few Famous Fliers from North Carolina 125

8. Some of North Carolina's Aviation Tragedies 147

9. Looking for North Carolina's Aviation Heritage: Museums and Static Displays 152

Appendix A: Tuskegee Airmen from North Carolina 165
Appendix B: Women's Air Service Pilots (WASP) from North Carolina 167
Appendix C: Lost Airports 169
Appendix D: Early North Carolina Landing Fields and Airports 173
Appendix E: 1940s North Carolina Air Carriers 175

Notes 177
Bibliography 193
Index 201
About the Author 207

PREFACE

On a windswept sand dune along North Carolina's Outer Banks sits a bronze and steel replica of the *Wright Flyer*. Orville Wright is represented lying on the bottom wing, while his brother Wilbur is running alongside, steadying the wing of the famous *Wright Flyer*. The 2003 memorial commemorates the first flight of humans in a heavier-than-air machine on December 17, 1903. While that flight was a historic event in itself, the invention of the airplane would alter world history in ways that the Wright brothers could not have foreseen. When Orville and Wilbur Wright returned to Ohio, the spark they had ignited grew into a flame that did not die. Others were interested in aviation as well. Innovators were always driven to build bigger and better airplanes, to improve airfields that eventually became international airports. As John Gillespie Magee Jr. wrote, they strove to slip "the surly bonds of Earth."

No other invention has revolutionized society the way the airplane has. Distant corners of the globe were opened to commerce; people were brought together across vast distances; different parts of the planet were explored; warfare was radically changed; and the foundation was laid for the exploration of space, the Moon and, in the future, other planets. In 2023, aviation was a $3.5 trillion worldwide industry, supporting 87.7 million jobs.[1]

North Carolina's role in this history goes far beyond the Wright brothers and Kitty Hawk. There were native Tar Heels fascinated with the idea of heavier-than-air powered flight, working on various designs for aeroplanes while Orville and Wilbur Wright tinkered with their own contraption on the coast. Some of these North Carolinians built their own planes. Others became pilots. The state became a stop for many of the famous fliers of the century: Lincoln Beachey, Wiley Post, Eddie Rickenbacker, Jimmy Doolittle, Paul Tibbets, Jacqueline Cochran, Amelia Earhart and Charles Lindbergh. At the same time, the state produced its own luminaries: Tiny Broadwick, Belvin W. Maynard, Warren Wheeler, George Preddy Jr., Robert Morgan, Tom Davis and Gus Shinn. Beyond these personalities, the state played a major role in aviation events, like the training of glider pilots and paratroopers for the invasion of Normandy during World War II.

This is the first attempt to compile a survey history of North Carolina's aviation history. There are numerous books on the Wright brothers. Thomas C. Parramore's *The First to Fly: North Carolina and the Beginnings of Aviation* (2002) admirably covers the history up to 1919. There are autobiographies by *Memphis Belle* pilot Robert Morgan and *Apollo 16* astronaut Charlie Duke, children's books on Tiny Broadwick, a couple of histories of Piedmont Airlines and a few other scattered books. For a state that proudly proclaims itself "First in Flight," there should be more. Hopefully, this project will spur others to more deeply examine different aspects of the story of aviation in North Carolina.

My own interest in aviation stems from my childhood. We often went to the closest airport to watch jets take off and land, and we even saw rockets blast off from time to time. In 2020, when I was working on *A History Lover's Guide to North Carolina*, I discovered this glaring gap in the state's historiography. Hopefully, this is a step in the right direction of filling this void.

There are some great people across the state of North Carolina and the nation who helped field questions and look for articles and photographs for this project. These individuals include Laurie Johnston, North Carolina Room, Burke County Public Library; Ann Haub, WASP Museum, Sweetwater, Texas; Alison Thurman and the great staff at the North Carolina Division of Archives and Records, Raleigh; the staff at the Robinson-Spangler Carolina Room, Charlotte Mecklenburg Library; the North Carolina Museum of History, Raleigh; and the Hickory Aviation Museum, Hickory. A very special thank-you to Elizabeth Baird Hardy. None of this would have been possible without her editing, proofing and listening to me when I say, "Hey, what do you think of this idea?"

1

BEFORE THE WRIGHT BROTHERS

EARLY AVIATION IN NORTH CAROLINA

Jules Verne made only one trip to the United States. It was 1867, and in a week, he explored New York City, Albany, Buffalo and Niagara Falls before returning to France. Despite the brevity of his trip, Verne often set his stories in the States. In 1904, he released *Master of the World.* In this novel, an inspector in the federal police department is sent to the Blue Ridge Mountains to investigate some strange occurrences. There, he finds Robur, who is bent on capturing the world. Inside a mountain along the Burke-McDowell County line, a base that contains a craft known as the *Terror* is discovered. This craft can operate as a boat, submarine, automobile or aircraft. While trying to escape the authorities, Robur heads toward the Caribbean, where the craft is struck by lightning and breaks apart.

Very few North Carolinians probably knew that Verne had located his villain's lair inside a mountain in the western part of the Tar Heel State. But thanks to newspapers, there were many across the state interested in the ability that Robur's vehicle had: to carry a person through the air like a bird.

There were a handful of North Carolinians exploring the idea of flight, long before the Wright brothers began tinkering. While the Chinese had used balloons and kites for at least two millennia, and Leonardo da Vinci had designed a device for mechanical flight, it was not until 1783 that three Frenchmen constructed a balloon in Paris, France, and used heated air to fly for forty-five minutes before landing. Before the end of the year, there were manned balloon flights. This was beginning of aviation. By 1785, accounts of balloon ascensions in Europe and New York were beginning to appear

The *Terror* flies over the Blue Ridge Mountains. *From* Master of the World.

in North Carolina newspapers. State newspapers followed the progress of these aeronauts from other places. It is unclear when the first balloon made its ascent over the Tar Heel State. It could have been flown by Vincent Dumilieu. Originally from France, Dumilieu toured the United States in the 1820s. A newspaper in Greensboro reported that on November 6, 1828, Dumilieu "raised a Balloon in this place....The Balloon was about 20 feet high and 45 in circumference—it ascended in fine style, until it attained about one mile in height, when it bore off majestically in a north eastern direction as far as the eye could see."[2]

Balloons slowly began to make appearances across the state. When the cornerstone was laid for the new capital building in Raleigh on July 4, 1833, a balloon ascension was a part of the festivities. Another balloon went up as part of Independence Day festivities in Raleigh in 1841. When President James K. Polk visited the capital in 1844, another balloon was launched. Fourth of July balloon ascensions became popular forms of entertainment. There was one in Tarboro in 1845 and others in Raleigh in 1846, Goldsboro in 1851, Wilmington in 1853 and Chapel Hill in 1854. Balloon launches seemed to be included in special events in every sizable town, including Asheville and Greensboro in 1851. A temperance demonstration in Salisbury that same year closed out the evening "by sending up a balloon in fine style." Following a Whig Party meeting in 1852 in Statesville, a balloon was sent up.[3]

Balloonist John Wise moved his operations from out of state to Wilmington in 1846. A newspaper reported that he had a long list of clients ready to ascend in his balloon. His "Arield Vessel" required 370 yards of silk and had a capacity of 48,000 gallons of hydrogen gas. Just seeing the balloon filled was "worth the price of admission." Tickets cost one dollar, with tickets for children and servants costing half the price. Several different locations sold tickets, and an omnibus ran from Market Street to the launching location. Wise stayed through the end of the year. "Professor" George Elliott was in Raleigh at the fairgrounds to exhibit balloon flights in December 1854. The first guest to ascend was reportedly a Mrs. McGinley, who soared to 50 or 100 yards, while tethered. Elliott's own flight was untethered, and he headed in a "southereasterly direction." At the time of this writing, it is not known where Elliot descended. Tickets just to watch cost fifty cents; children's tickets cost twenty-five cents.[4]

As the nineteenth century progressed, the idea of heavier-than-air mechanized flight appeared from time to time. In 1832, a Charlotte newspaper reprinted a piece from London regarding drawings of steam engines moving balloons through the air. While the London editor doubted mechanized flight would ever happen, there had already been achievements in science during the past "three quarters of a century" that made it "really difficult to fix any limits to their future conquests." Other state newspapers reported additional projects, mostly out-of-state ventures, in which intrepid inventors were trying to build flying machines. One man in New Orleans was building a "vast kite, with machinery attached underneath to navigate it with." In Baltimore, there were experiments with a "steam balloon," and in Boston, Captain Taggart was working on a balloon with "flying machine attached." By the early 1890s, Samuel P. Langley's work on a flying machine occupied many columns of newsprint.[5]

The idea of a flying machine was not just some far-flung notion from wacky inventors. It was a concept embraced by a handful of North Carolinians. *The Charlotte Observer* reported in January 1878 that Dr. Asbury was designing an "air boat" that used a lightweight fixed wing and treadles. Professor Beard, as reported in the *Greensboro Patriot* in November 1883, was also working on a machine. Hertford County's James H. Gatling, in the 1870s, constructed a heavier-than-air monoplane of light poplar, with white oak split wings held together by wire. It had a front elevator that caused the nose to go up and down, a vertical rudder and tricycle-style landing gear. Gatling's machine had no engine and used human power alone, its premise being that less power would be necessary once it was airborne. According to legend, it flew just once in 1873. Gatling was pushed off a twelve-foot-high platform, and while he cranked furiously, the craft crashed shortly thereafter. Gatling never flew again, although his aircraft survived in a shed until a fire in 1905.[6]

Jacob Hill of Stokes County was reportedly working on a flying machine in the spring of 1901. He was in Winston-Salem in May with a diagram of the machine, looking for investors. While several local businessmen had subscribed to the project, it was reported that Hill, in late November, went looking for Northern capitalists. Hill announced that he was planning to enter a flying contest in St. Louis in 1904, a contest with a $200,000 prize. A Winston-Salem firm, Hege Brothers, was hired to build a model in 1902. The device was described as having balloons, with a "cigar-shaped car" underneath. On either side of the car were two "large rotary fans" powered by an electric motor with batteries. Steering was accomplished using a propellor. If the model was a success, then a full-scale craft was to be built. Hill's flying machine generated great interest in the press. Work was completed on the model by May 1902, and Hill sought to organize a stock company to build the full-size machine. In July, it was reported that he was returning to Stokes County to work "on a real flying machine as soon as the required capital stock of $1,000 is subscribed."[7]

While the state was watching a world that dreamed of flying and creating often-fantastical concepts, two unassuming brothers from Ohio quietly worked to make human flight a reality. Their efforts finally paid off on a cold December day on a sand dune on the coast of North Carolina.

2

TWELVE SECONDS AT KITTY HAWK

Like the rest of the nation, North Carolinians were fascinated with the exploits of Samuel P. Langley, a self-taught astronomer, physicist and secretary of the Smithsonian Institution. In May 1896, he launched a steam-powered, unpiloted model aircraft that flew just over half a mile down the Potomac River. The problem with its design was power. Steam engines were heavy and required wood or coal fuel and water. Regardless, North Carolina newspapers from Statesville to Edenton were quick to record Langley's success, along with the endeavors of others like Octave Chanute. In 1891, the *Asheville Daily Citizen* copied an article titled "We Shall Yet Fly," which mentions Langley and aviation pioneer Chanute and claims that the "study of aeronautics is no longer confined to ridiculed cranks."[8]

Two brothers in Ohio, Orville and Wilbur Wright, were fascinated by the plethora of articles on various aviation ventures that were circulating in the press across the nation. They owned a bicycle shop in Dayton and were described as exhibiting "a decided curiosity about the world around them and a capacity to solve problems through experimentation." They designed and built a machine to fold church bulletins, their own printing press and their own bicycles. The challenges of human flight likewise captured their attention. In 1899, Wilbur wrote to the Smithsonian Institute, asking for copies of any papers it had published on aviation. After reading the available material, the brothers decided to build their own glider-kite, which they flew near their home that August.[9]

Dayton did not have the reliable winds needed to test the glider. In November, Wilbur wrote the U.S. Weather Bureau to ask about wind velocities in the Chicago area. The agent sent copies of the *Monthly Weather Review*, which contained information on each of the weather stations in the United States. The brothers needed wind, but they also needed sand for soft landings. Wilbur wrote to the head of the Weather Bureau at Kitty Hawk to ask about the conditions. William J. "Bill" Tate, postmaster and assistant weatherman, wrote back, stating that the area contained "a strech [*sic*] of sandy beach 1 mile [wide] by five [long] with a bare hill in the center 80 feet high not a tree or bush any where.... [O]ur winds are always steady generally from 10 to 20 miles [an hour]." Wilbur was on his way to the Outer Banks by September the following year. He took a train to Elizabeth City and then a boat to Kitty Hawk. Soon, his baggage arrived along with a crate containing the glider. While boarding with the Tate family, Wilbur assembled the glider. The white French sateen had to be cut and resewn due to a lack of eighteen-foot-long spruce spars (Wilbur had been able to find only seventeen-foot-long pine locally). Orville arrived later, and the brothers relocated to Lookout Hill. The glider was tethered to a wooden derrick, and then later, the two Wrights and Tate held it. However, it did not perform as they had envisioned. They even added eleven-year-old Tom Tate as a ballast and moved to an even higher hill—Big Kill Devil Hill—where Wilbur himself attempted free flights on October 19. Flights of three hundred and four hundred yards were recorded. Toward the end of October, the Wrights were on their way back to Ohio. The original glider, now wrecked, was given to Bill Tate. The cloth from the wings was used by the family to make dresses for Tate's daughters, and he used the wood to fashion tools for his farm.[10]

Back in Dayton, the brothers took what they had learned and constructed a new glider. In July 1901, they returned to Kitty Hawk. Land around Kill Devil Hills was leased to them; a combination hangar, shop and sleeping quarters was constructed; and a well was drilled for fresh water. The brothers also had company. Edward Huffaker arrived with a disassembled glider that Octave Chanute had sponsored, along with George A. Spratt, a former medical student whom Chanute had also recommended. On July 27, experimental flights resumed with disappointing results. The wings were cambered incorrectly. After several days of reworking the wings, test flights began again. By August 20, the team, which at times included Chanute, were all on their way back to their homes, disappointed with the tests. Orville wrote years later that Wilbur asserted, "Not in a thousand years would man ever fly."[11]

The 1903 *Wright Flyer* sits in the sand at Kill Devil Hills. *Library of Congress.*

Over the next few months, the brothers began to rework the mathematics involved in the wings. They even built their own wind tunnel to test numerous wing designs. In September 1902, they returned to Kitty Hawk, where they revamped their camp and constructed their largest glider to date. On September 19, their experiments commenced. In early October, Orville had the idea to make the rudder movable. Work began on the improvements. This improvement allowed them to glide for more than six hundred feet along the North Carolina beach. They returned to Dayton with new knowledge and experience—and the desire to build an engine.[12]

Word of their experiments leaked out in October 1902, when a newspaper in Elizabeth City reported, "Noted Inventors Are Making a Flying Machine at Kitty Hawk." The Wright brothers, along with others, including Chanute, were "on the bleak sands…laboring arduously in the perfection of a flying machine." They were currently experimenting with a glider "with a number of silken wings and steering attachments.…With this frail contrivance the aeronaut leaps from the crest of the highest sand dune…and borne up on the wind, he steers his queer craft right or left, goes downward or upward until the velocity of the wind abates and compels a descent." The next summer, the editor reported, the team planned to attach an electric motor

The 1903 *Wright Flyer* can be seen next to the camp building where it was housed. The smaller building was used by the Wrights as a workshop and living quarters. *Library of Congress.*

and propellor to the glider to "vie with the birds in flight: defying gravitation and adverse winds." The article was reprinted in a handful of newspapers, including those in Raleigh and Minneapolis.[13]

With the brothers spending weeks away from their shop every year testing in Kitty Hawk, Charlie Taylor was hired to keep the bicycle shop running. He was described as a "brilliant mechanic." When queries to manufacturers about automobile engines did not produce the desired results, Taylor set out to build one. The end product was a four-cylinder, cast-aluminum block engine without a carburetor that produced twelve horsepower and weighed less than 160 pounds. Next came propellers, which Taylor and the Wrights also designed. The new *Flyer* had two eight-foot-long laminated spruce propellers, handmade with a hatchet and spokeshave; one turned clockwise, and the other turned counterclockwise, driven by chains.

Local residents welcomed the Wright brothers back to Kitty Hawk in September 1903. A new building was constructed at Kill Devil Hills to house the new craft. At first, the new *Flyer* was used to perform glider tests. In early November, the engine was installed. However, a misfiring engine damaged the propellers, and they had to be sent back to Ohio for repairs. While they waited, the Wrights fine-tuned the engine and built a single track the *Flyer* would move down when it came time to launch. When replacement propellers arrived, the new, larger, steel-tube props cracked when tested. Orville returned to Dayton to work on replacements and returned to Kitty Hawk on December 11.

December 17 was a cold day in the Outer Banks. Nearby ponds were covered in ice, and a bitter wind blew from the north. The Wrights, with the help of men nearby, hauled the *Flyer* to the launch track. Orville had won a coin toss between the brothers to determine who would make the first flight attempt. He climbed up on the *Flyer* and lay down on his stomach between the wings. At 10:35 a.m., after the engine warmed up, the rope holding back the *Flyer* was released, and the craft slowly moved down the track and into the air. The flight lasted approximately twelve seconds and covered 120 feet. While it was brief, "it was a real flight at last," Orville later said. Wilbur flew that afternoon, covering 175 feet, and then Orville flew again, covering 200 feet. About noon, Wilbur flew for a little over half a mile, a flight that lasted fifty-nine seconds. The brothers were considering another flight when a gust of wind caught the *Flyer*, along with John T. Daniels, and sent it tumbling down the beach. Daniels escaped with some scratches and bruises, but the *Flyer* was wrecked. That afternoon, the brothers walked four miles up the beach to send a telegram home, announcing their triumph.[14]

The press was largely ignorant of the success of the Wright brothers. Orville and Wilbur had purposely operated out of the spotlight while working on their *Flyer*. The press was focused on Langley's Aerodrome. It

The first flight lasted twelve seconds and covered 120 feet. *Library of Congress.*

had cost nearly $70,000, mostly through taxpayer funds. A catapult was built on a houseboat in the Potomac River for the launch. Two attempted flights on October 7 and December 8 were unsuccessful, with the pilot, Charles Manley, dunked in the river. State newspapers were quick to note the failure of Langley's Aerodrome. The attempt resulted in the "complete wreck of the airship," stated *The Wilmington Messenger*. "Langley's Dream Develops the Qualities of a Duck," ran the front page of Raleigh's *News and Observer*.[15]

Within North Carolina, the press was unaware of what had actually transpired on the state's coast. Only the *Norfolk Virginia-Pilot* carried the Wrights' story, a story the brothers asked the telegraph operator to keep confidential. Raleigh's *The Morning Post* and the *Goldsboro Weekly Argus* picked it up from the Virginia newspaper and reprinted the article on December 23 and December 24, respectively. It read:

> *Norfolk, VA., Dec. 22—Norville* [sic] *and Wilbur Wright, the inventors of the dirigible flyer, passed through here to-night going to Dayton, O. They assert that they have made seven successful trials of their flyer in three weeks and that they will give a public exhibition at home. The trials were made at Kitty Hawk on the North Carolina coast. The Wrights declare the flyer maintained its height and traveled at will even in strong winds within a radius of half a mile. They are confident of half a mile. They are confident of the success of their invention and declare that the trials at Kitty Hawk have demonstrated the practicability of the aeroplane idea, on which they have worked for years.*[16]

A formal statement was released to the press in early January, and it was picked up by newspapers in Wilmington, Raleigh, Charlotte, Greensboro, Windsor and Mt. Airy. *The Asheville Gazette News* went into further detail, featuring a woodcut image of both the *Flyer* and the brothers. Orville and Wilbur had "eclipsed as air navigators" those with dirigible balloons. "The Wright flier has no balloon attachment of any kind, but is supported in the air by a pair of…wings." The article went on to describe the construction of the aircraft, its weight and how it worked. Then a history of the work of the Wrights since 1901, including their various gliders and trials, was recounted.[17]

Wilbur Wright did not return to Kitty Hawk until April 1908. The brothers' testing of new machines had moved to Huffman Prairie near Dayton, Ohio. These new aircraft were spending more time in the air and flying faster. Patents were issued for the new aircraft, and the brothers traveled to Europe to sell their planes in France. When the U.S. Signal Corps advertised bids for a heavier-than-air military aeroplane, the brothers submitted a bid, which was accepted. They returned to Kitty Hawk to brush up on their flying skills for the upcoming test. On arrival, Wilbur rebuilt the camp, which had been destroyed by storms and vandals. Orville soon arrived, and work began to uncrate the new *Flyer*. One of its many improvements was its ability to carry two people, sitting side by side. This time, their work was besieged by reporters, who often observed from a distance. On May 14, Charles W. Furnas boarded the plane with Wilbur, and for the first time, two people flew together. Not long thereafter, Wilbur was on his way to France and Orville to Fort Myers, Virginia, for flying demonstrations. There were many highs and lows for the Wright brothers over the next few years. Orville was seriously injured in a crash at Fort Myers, and his passenger was killed. Wilbur won the Michelin Cup in 1908 with a flight that lasted two hours and eighteen minutes and covered more than seventy-six miles. The pair was awarded a Congressional Medal in March 1909, "in recognition of the great service of Orville and Wilbur Wright, of Ohio, rendered the science of aerial navigation in the invention of the Wright aeroplane, and for their ability, courage, and success in navigating the air." The brothers also went through lawsuits, like the one they brought against Glenn H. Curtiss for patent infringement. In 1910, Orville began training pilots for the Wright Exhibition Company, which flew its first show in Indianapolis, Indiana, in June that year. Wilbur died of typhoid fever in Dayton on May 30, 1912. In 1915, Orville sold the company, and the next year, it merged with the Glenn L. Martin Company to become the Wright-Martin Aircraft Corporation, with Orville as its chief consulting engineer. President Woodrow Wilson appointed Orville as a member of the National Advisory Committee for Aeronautics in 1920, and he served until his death in 1948.

Orville visited Kitty Hawk again in October 1911 to fly gliders. Some believe that Orville made at least three—and maybe as many as six—other trips to the area after the brothers' 1911 visit. He attended the December 1928 event to celebrate the twenty-fifth anniversary of that first flight and lay the cornerstone for the future monument. Amelia Earhart was at that ceremony. Orville's last official visit to Kitty Hawk came when he attended the dedication of the Kill Devil Hill National Memorial in November 1932.[18]

It was announced in 1925 that the original *Wright Flyer* would be sent to London for exhibition. The choice of London, rather than an American site, was the result of a dispute between the Wrights and the Smithsonian Institute. The Wrights had attempted to donate the *Wright Flyer* to the

Smithsonian in 1910. Then–Smithsonian Secretary Charles Walcott demurred, as he wanted a newer model to be displayed next to Langley's Aerodrome. The 1903 *Wright Flyer* was packed away in a shed in Dayton and displayed from time to time, such as at the dedication of new buildings at the Massachusetts Institute of Technology in 1916, the Pan-American Aeronautical Exhibition in New York in 1917, the Aeronautical Exposition in New York in 1919 and the International Air Races in Dayton in 1924. Back in Washington, D.C., the Smithsonian hired Glenn Curtiss to rebuild Langley's Aerodrome. Curtiss installed a new engine and modified the aircraft and was able to make some straight-line, brief hops with the craft. It was returned to the Smithsonian and displayed as the "first-man carrying aeroplane in the history of the world capable of sustained flight." Orville sent the original *Wright Flyer* to the Science Museum in London, hoping to create an uproar when the first aircraft designed and built by Americans in America was being displayed in England, not America. There was public outcry, even in North Carolina. W.O. Saunders, an Elizabeth City editor and president of the Kill Devil Hills Memorial Association, went to visit Orville in an attempt to get the historic craft displayed in the state museum in Raleigh. Orville acknowledged the request and replied that for the past ten years, the Ohio State Museum in Columbus had been attempting to get the *Flyer*: "I have thought the machine only ought to go into a museum having a good reputation of the art of which it is a part. None of the State museums of the country has this." Getting the *Wright Flyer* back came up from time to time. In April 1930, the press related an attempt to get the plane back to the Smithsonian. The Wilmington Chamber of Commerce sent a letter to its congressional representative in February 1933, asking that steps be taken to get the machine returned. "The reason" the famous airplane was in London and not in Washington, D.C., was "that the Smithsonian has distorted the history of aviation so as to deny Orville Wright and the late Wilbur Wright recognition as the inventors of the first successful flying-machine," opined the editor of a Chapel Hill newspaper. With the advent of the Second World War, the historic craft was boxed up and moved for safekeeping. North Carolina's Governor Broughton appealed to Orville in December 1942, asking that the artifact be returned to the United States and placed in a special museum in Kitty Hawk. Orville and the leadership at the Smithsonian finally came to terms, and in 1943, he agreed to bring the *Wright Flyer* back to the States. Orville died of a heart attack in January 1948. The original *Wright Flyer* went on display in the Smithsonian on December 17, 1948, forty-five years after making that first flight.[19]

Two Boeing B-29s fly over the Wright Brothers Memorial in December 1949 during the forty-sixth annual commemoration of the first flight. *United States Air Force.*

While the accomplishments of the Wright brothers just south of Kitty Hawk at Kill Devil Hills were due to their hard work, they had an abundance of help from local people. When they first arrived, the home of Bill Tate became their base until a tent could be pitched or structures built or repaired. Addie Tate loaned Wilbur her treadle sewing machine so he could alter the original glider. Joe Dosher from the Weather Bureau station loaned the brothers an anemometer to measure wind speed. Various members of the nearby lifesaving station helped at times, including Surfman John Daniels, who took a photograph of the first flight. Another crewmember at the lifesaving station, Adam Etheridge, was hired to look after the buildings at the camp.[20]

Despite the humble beginnings of flight on an isolated stretch of beach in North Carolina, the yearning to soar with the birds would soon take hold the world over.

3

BARNSTORMING AND AERIAL COMBAT

1909–1918

It is unlikely that William Luther Paul and the Wright brothers ever met. Born in Carteret County in 1869, Paul was known for having "an uncanny ability to mend tools and machines"; plus, he was able to conceive and construct new inventions. Paul built his own bicycle, a block and tackle system for moving bricks while building a chimney and a mobile movie theater that traveled via water. As early as 1903, Paul claimed he was experimenting with a flying machine. One of Paul's inventions was the *Bumble Bee*. Using a motorcycle engine (or maybe four motorcycle engines) and two four-blade rotors, eight feet in diameter, the *Bumble Bee* was a helicopter rather than a glider. In 1907, an unmanned and tethered *Bumble Bee*, Paul claimed, sailed four or five feet off the ground inside a specially constructed hangar. There were witnesses, and the experiment was performed several times, at least once with sixty pounds of weight added. Paul was planning to fly himself when his wife convinced him to abandon the project. She had read of a crash, possibly the one involving Orville Wright in September 1908, in which the passenger was killed. If Paul's claims are true, he could possibly have achieved some form of powered—albeit unmanned—flight prior to the success of the Wright brothers.[21]

Had the Wright brothers built the research center on the Outer Banks as they had discussed, then North Carolina might have become the aviation capital of the world. Although the state missed out on this designation, North Carolinians were still fascinated with aviation. In the fall of 1908, one of the Charles J. Strobel flying machines made its way around the fairs in Raleigh, Charlotte, Salisbury and Greensboro. Strobel's airships were composed of a balloon with a spot for a pilot underneath, and they were powered by a four-cylinder gasoline engine. Lincoln Beachey, the "World's Greatest Aviation Pioneer," piloted the airship in Raleigh and Charlotte, while Charles Hamilton assumed the controls in Greensboro. In Charlotte, where the cost to bring the aircraft to the fair was $1,500, weather grounded the craft for a couple of days. One of the advertised flights was done at night, with searchlights used to follow the craft. In Greensboro, the first flight lasted twenty minutes, with the airship circling over the fairgrounds several times. The late afternoon flight lasted an hour, with Hamilton "sailing" over Greensboro.[22]

Ballooning continued to be a popular attraction at county fairs through the nineteenth century and well into the twentieth, with an added twist: the addition of parachutes. In July 1858, it was advertised that Monsieur Morat would make a balloon ascent at the Shoco Springs Resort in Warren County, and a "quadruped will be let down in a parachute from a height of 2,000 feet." Morat went up on July 29, and the small dog sailed safely to "mother earth in a few minutes…uninjured." It appears that human balloonists themselves did not begin making parachute drops in North Carolina until 1888. The fairs in Raleigh and Greensboro both advertised that a "well-known aeronaut" would parachute from a balloon, "a sight but few of our people have ever witnessed." By 1900, a parachute drop by an "aeronaut" was a regular occurrence at county fairs and circuses, with reports of such amusements at New Bern, Greenville, Asheville, Lumberton, Youngsville, Mt. Holly, Greensboro, Littleton, North Wilkesboro, Winston-Salem, Franklin, Kinston, Weldon and Raleigh.[23]

Often, the balloonists traveled in teams. In New Bern in October 1900, the team of Professor Hutchinson and Miss Tetta Danzelle was performing. One aeronaut would ascend in the balloon and jump, while the other remained on the ground to control the tethered balloon. The act could be dangerous. At the 1889 fair in Mt. Holly, W.R. Perry's balloon burst as he was going up. At only seven hundred feet above the ground, he was unable to deploy his parachute and fell. He died as a result of his injuries a couple of days later. The danger did not deter some from wanting to follow them into the air. Georgia Thompson was a teenage mother from Granville County when she visited a carnival in Raleigh, probably in April 1908. There, she witnessed "Sig. and Senorita Brodricks, French Aeronauts, in their Startling and Thrilling Double Balloon Ascension." Known as "Tiny" due to her small size, Thompson decided that sailing from a balloon with a parachute was something she wanted to pursue. The balloonist was the famed Charles Broadwick, who was himself designing his own parachutes when he was a teenager in the 1880s. Tiny joined Broadwick and made jumps as early as August 1908, when it was reported that Tiny had already jumped at a carnival in Morganton and was billed at the upcoming fair in Statesville. In time, she adopted Charles Broadwick's last name and was billed as Tiny Broadwick, or "The Doll Girl," due to her size and age. While performing with Broadwick, she sat on a trapeze under the balloon as it ascended. When the balloon reached its zenith and began to sink, she would leap from her perch and float to the ground.

Tiny was the first woman to parachute from an airplane, piloted by Glenn Martin, in Chicago in September 1912; the first woman to parachute into a body of water, jumping into Lake Michigan in 1914; and the first person to parachute from a seaplane.[24]

Many across the state were catching the "aeroplane" fever. Newspapers ran articles almost daily of flights in France, England, Los Angeles and New York. Inspired by all of these accounts, a handful of North Carolinians were ready to take to the skies. One historian believes that between mid-1910 and early 1912, at least a dozen audacious aviators constructed aircraft, while at least eleven more tried and failed, all within the Tar Heel State. Wilmingtonian David Palmgren founded the American Aeroplane Company in the late summer of 1909, with other Wilmington businessmen as stockholders. Working out of a shop and hangar at Castle Hayne, Palmgren named his craft the *American*. It had a thirty-foot-long tubular steel fuselage with two thirty-six-foot-long wings. There were propellers both fore and aft, with two 50-horsepower engines, a sixty-five-gallon fuel tank and room for twelve passengers if they stood. The *American* was displayed at the Grand Central Palace in New York in May 1912. Palmgren's plans popped up in the newspaper from time to time, but it is unclear if his airplane ever left the ground. Two other men with ties to Wilmington, Harold Chase and Minor Gouverneur, were also working on an airplane. Their location was Shell Island, only accessible by boat. The plane was described as being thirty feet long and sixteen feet wide, with a 250-horsepower engine, which was later replaced by a smaller, lighter 40-horsepower engine. They might have flown as early as June 20, 1910, when a local man reported seeing a craft pass over the city, but it was not until November that official word was published that Chase and Gouverneur were making successful flights. That year, the pair also applied for two different patents for steering mechanisms. Chase moved on

An early military bomber is inspected by a crowd at Pinehurst. *Author's collection.*

to other ventures, but Gouverneur continued to work on various airplanes through at least 1912.[25]

There were aviation schemes and ideas all over the state. Companies were founded in Charlotte and Durham to build airplanes. In Weaverville, R.S. Howland built his own biplane. At the same time, Raymond Allison of Statesville went to Boston to learn to fly. There were also traveling exhibits, like the one in Goldsboro where an airplane was set up in the opera house.[26]

With seemingly bated breath, North Carolinians watched the great aviation meets in other states, along with races that were being run in Europe. Business promoters kept asking the question, "Why not here?" The first aviation meet in North Carolina was held in Charlotte. High winds prevented J.A. McCurdy from taking to the air on November 10 and November 11, but the Curtiss biplane made two flights on November 12. "The sight was thrillingly beautiful as the machine left the ground and floated away," wrote the editor of the *Charlotte News*, the promoter of the event. "Southward it went over the fence and as high, or higher than the tree tops. Then a turn was made that was as graceful as a bird on the wing. Back to the field it came lighting safely on an even keel." As the plane was landing after the second flight, the wind caught the craft and wrecked it. Raleigh held the next aviation meet about a week after the event in Charlotte. The fairgrounds were the site of the event that also featured Curtiss biplanes. Numerous individuals submitted letters asking for a ride in one of the airplanes. One advertised feature of the event was a race between one of the airplanes and an automobile. The car was driven by Mrs. H.D. Wolcott, and the ensuing crash of the car into the crowd, which resulted in the deaths of two people, marred the event. Goldsboro attempted an aviation meet at the end of November, which featured Blériot monoplanes flown in from Revilo Park. The exhibition was plagued with problems, which started when the airplanes failed to arrive on the train. When one did arrive and was assembled, it crashed just a few seconds after takeoff, depriving the crowds of the show. Winston-Salem hosted another aviation meet before the end of the month. The event featured two pilots who flew Curtiss biplanes based out of Piedmont Park. The "professional bird men" were "complete masters of the wonderful craft....Every landing was made with the ease of a great bird and almost in the same spot each time." One thousand people witnessed the flights, which lasted about seven minutes each. At the end, one of the pilots faced off against one of the local militia companies, the Forsyth Riflemen. The militiamen fired blanks at the pilot while he dropped bombs composed of bags of flour. The two pilots were treated to dinner at Hotel Zinzendorf that evening.[27]

Wilmington held the first aviation meet of 1911, with pilots J.A. McCurdy and Lincoln Beachey. After Beachey took off from the airport, his flight over Wilmington lasted eleven minutes. Beachey, deemed the world's first stunt pilot and "The World's Greatest Aviator," went to Pinehurst next, and he stayed there for three weeks. The local newspaper confessed that golf had taken a backseat to airplane demonstrations. It also appears that Beachey visited Greensboro, Winston-Salem and Asheville in April and Durham in May. Charles Evans Jr., on taking flight for the first time from Pinehurst, thought that he would be afraid, the "awesome sort of fear which assails a boy on passing a cemetery on a dark night." Instead, he said, "As we rose into the air, hovering gently as it seemed above the pine woods, a profound sensation of security came over me, and while the rush of air was tremendous and the revolutions of the high-power motor deafening, I felt as safe as if sitting upon a sheltered balcony." After his travels north that summer, which included a flight under the bridge near Niagara Falls and others that broke altitude records, Beachey returned to North Carolina. He flew at the state fair in Raleigh in October, at the fair in High Point and at an aviation meet in Salisbury in November. Beachey died in a crash at the Panama-Pacific International Exposition San Francisco in March 1915.[28]

In the early 1900s, every county fair wanted a balloon. A decade later, with companies like Wright, Curtiss, Glenn Martin, Blériot and many others

Top: Lincoln Beachey was the first widely known aviator to visit North Carolina, offering tours and exhibition flying for the public. *Library of Congress.*

Bottom: Golf took a backseat to aviation when Lincoln Beachey flew into Pinehurst in 1911. *Author's collection.*

manufacturing airplanes, the demand for the craft at county and regional fairs soared. Fairs were not the only events that included feats in the air. Airplanes flew over Charlotte during the Mecklenburg Declaration of Independence celebration in 1912. Both Lumberton's and Shelby's Fourth of July festivals in 1913 featured two airplanes, as did the festival at Guilford Courthouse Battleground the next year. The fairgrounds at most county fairs provided enough room for pilots to take off and land although, at times, it could be a little tight. When in the air, pilots did more than just circle the landing fields. At the fair in New Bern in 1914, the airplanes raced automobiles and took up passengers (famed photographer Baynard Wooten was one of those registered to take a flight), and pilots dropped dummy hand grenades at targets. At the state fair that year in Raleigh, "Dr. Lloyd Thompson" toyed with death "in his marvelous feat of looping in an aeroplane in the air…something never before witnessed in this State." With the beginning of World War I in Europe, the dummy hand grenades were upgraded to dummy bombs. The fairs in both Gastonia and Raleigh in 1915 featured airplanes that "bombed" forts or targets below.[29]

There were also the beginnings of legal battles in the 1910s regarding various aviation endeavors. In January 1915, the Price Aviation Company was in Wilmington with a Wright Hydroplane. The craft was moored in the Cape Fear River at Sunset Park. Price Aviation was contracted to give tours, race another hydroplane and drop "bombs" during exhibitions, with the proceeds going to the local Red Cross tuberculosis sanitarium. However, pilot Howard Rinehart struggled to get the hydroplane out of the water. The owners of Sunset Park sued for $1,125.40 for breach of contract, and the New Hanover County sheriff seized the aircraft. By mid-February, the dispute was settled and the hydroplane returned. In Greensboro, North Carolina, A&M student Forrest Wysong was charged with obtaining money under a false pretense. Wysong was hired to construct a plane for Stephen Bruner. The aircraft was constructed in the shops of the college, and Wysong took it for a flight in 1915. Shortly thereafter, he was summoned to the college president's office, where his father, who had forbidden him from flying, sat. Wysong and his brother Paul had previously built a glider, which crashed on its first flight. Bruner's deal with Wysong was that the latter would fly at fairs and festivals to make money for the company. Wysong agreed to turn over the airplane to Bruner. When Bruner arrived in Greensboro to recover his airplane, it was nowhere to be found. Friends of Wysong had boxed up the craft and stored it in the college foundry building, with plans to ship it to Wysong's lawyer.

Wysong and his lawyer claimed to have no knowledge of the event, and the crate was turned over to Bruner.[30]

In early 1917, the general assembly passed the first aviation law in North Carolina. The coastal area of the state had long been a haven for duck and geese hunting, drawing hunters from surrounding states. Some aviators were using their airplanes to stampede "the ducks and putting the land and boat hunters out of business." The law prohibited pilots or their passengers from "shooting, chasing, pursing, or harassing wild ducks, geese, swan or other wild water-fowl in and upon the sounds, rivers, creeks, or bays." Fines for those convicted were between $100 and $500 or not more than six months in prison.[31]

After designing, building and flying the first successful airplane, the Wright brothers believed the U.S. military would be a primary customer. At first, the U.S. Army turned them down, and it was not until 1908 that the first military trials took place at Fort Myers in Virginia. The U.S. Army finally accepted the airplane in August 1909. There were some who believed that an airplane would never have a role in warfare. Others predicted aircraft would become as indispensable as rifles, machine guns and tanks. When the smoldering embers of discontent flamed into World War I across Europe, the United States managed to stay out of the fight for several years. Despite the isolationist attitude of American politicians, the press across North Carolina and other states carried articles seemingly every time an Allied airplane took off and bombed enemy lines or saw an opposing aircraft. That military-focused coverage crowded out much of the aircraft development news across North Carolina.[32]

While the United States attempted to stay out of the fight, there were a handful of citizens who boarded ships to cross the Atlantic and look for places to enlist. As foreigners, they were not allowed to join the regular French army. Some, like brothers Kiffin and Paul Rockwell, joined the French Foreign Legion instead. Kiffin was born in Tennessee, but after his father died, the family returned to North Carolina. The brothers grew up in Asheville. By October 1914, they were in the trenches. Paul was wounded so badly that winter that he was forced out of the army. Kiffin transferred to the French Aviation Service in September 1915. The Lafayette Escadrille was composed of volunteer American aviators under French officers. On May 18, 1916, Kiffin was flying a Nieuport N11 on patrol when he spotted a German plane below him. Kiffin fired on the airplane, becoming the first American aviator to shoot down an enemy aircraft. He downed a second German fighter on May 24, despite being wounded in the process. Less than

Aviator Kiffin Yates Rockwell sits in the cockpit of his French Nieuport XI airplane in the Verdun sector of France in July 1916. *State Archives of North Carolina.*

twenty-four hours later, Kiffin was in the air again. Kiffin was credited with four aerial victories. Three days after his twenty-fourth birthday, Kiffin was engaged with a German Albatros when he was struck and killed, crashing into a field near the town of Rodern.[33]

Rockwell was not the only North Carolina aviator who flew in France. Arthur Bluethenthal, a Jewish Wilmington native and coach at the University of North Carolina, flew a bomber in Escadrille 227. While directing artillery fire above the battle near Marseillaise, he was shot down by German fighters. His remains were returned to Wilmington. James H. Baugham hailed from Beaufort County, played football at what is now North Carolina State University and earned his pilot's license from the Curtiss Aviation School in New York. Too young to serve as an aviator in the U.S. military, Baugham joined the Escadrille 157, a part of the Lafayette Escadrille, in December 1917 and later transferred to Escadrille 98. After a year of service in France, Baugham was mortally wounded while he engaged three German fighters. Some believe that Baugham was shot down by Ernst Udet, the second highest-scoring German ace of World War I, after Manfred von Richthofen, the so-called Red Baron. North Carolina's James R. McConnell lived in Carthage prior to joining the Lafayette Escadrille. McConnell was wounded in a crash and spent time in a French hospital. He had to persuade the hospital staff to allow him to return to the front, and seven days later, on

March 19, 1917, he was killed while he engaged German fighters over the Somme. McConnell was buried in France.[34]

Once the United States entered the war in April 1917, there were other North Carolina aviators who took to the skies, including Rockingham County's Robert O. Lindsay, an ace assigned to the 139th Aero Squadron credited with bringing down six enemy airplanes. Anson County's Lieutenant Belvin Maynard tested aircraft while he was stationed in France. Rowan County's Lieutenant James J. Sykes, 1st Aero Squadron, was shot down behind enemy lines in August 1918. Wilson County's Lieutenant John C. Lumsden, 12th Aero Squadron, was killed on July 28, 1918. Ensign Junius Andrews, from Chatham County, was a naval aviator who died in a seaplane accident in July 1918. Wilmington native Harmon C. Rorison served in the 22nd Aero Squadron and was credited with downing three enemy aircraft.

As the war raged overseas and tens of thousands of North Carolinians were shipped off to the mangled landscape of France, aviation within the state ground to a halt. Accounts of aircraft at fairs and festivals just about ceased. Instead, the attention of the state became focused on wartime activity. Several military bases were established, including Camp Polk in Raleigh, Camp Bragg near Fayetteville and Camp Greene in Charlotte.

Aviators of the Lafayette Escadrille are pictured at the Béhonne Airfield in the Verdun area of France in August 1916. *Left to right*: Lieutenant Alfred de Laage de Meux, Chouteau Johnson, Lawrence Rumsey, James R. McConnell, William Thaw, Raoul Lufbery, Kiffin Yates Rockwell, Didier Masson and Norman Prince. *State Archives of North Carolina.*

Residents in Carthage honor local LaFayette Escadrille member James R. McConnell, who was killed in France during World War I. *Author's collection.*

At its peak, Camp Greene hosted forty-one thousand troops and was the largest camp in North Carolina during the war. Authorization by the War Department for an "Aviation Center" at Camp Greene came in May 1918. Due to Camp Greene's topography, which resembled the rolling countryside of France, its aviation base was to provide the final training for pilots who were heading overseas. In June, an aviation recruiting office was opened at the camp. New recruits had to be between the ages of eighteen and forty-one and had to be registered for military service. There was a long list of new positions that were advertised; the military needed mechanics, radio operators, electricians, instrument repairmen, cabinetmakers, armorers, sail makers, photographers, machinists, rope riggers, propeller makers, vulcanizers, welders, and more. In mid-June, it was reported that aircraft had been boxed up and sent via the railroad to Camp Greene. Five Curtiss planes were shipped in from Gerstner Field, and six other aircraft came in from Love Field. Various Curtiss and Hall Scott motors were also shipped in. They were used to train mechanics and riggers. By the end of the month, those craft had begun arriving at the camp. Eventually, four aero squadrons were organized at Camp Greene: the 306th, 307th, 308th and 310th. All four spent time in Europe between July 1918 and December 1918. It appears that after these squadrons left for Europe, the aviation training facility at Camp Greene was closed.[35]

Camp Glenn, located near Morehead City, was another facility used during World War I. The base started as a training facility for the North Carolina National Guard. In 1916, men who were heading to fight against Pancho Villa along the country's border with Mexico were mobilized at Camp Glenn. With German U-boat activity along the coast, including the sinking of the *Diamond Shoals* lightship and two other vessels in August 1918, the navy established a naval air station at the base, transferring one plane and 8 men to the site. Later, twelve Curtiss airplanes and 320 men were stationed at Camp Glenn, charged with patrolling the coast as far south as Charleston. The coast guard took over the base in the 1920s, flying Curtiss seaplanes on patrol and performing test rescues of sailors.[36]

North Carolina provided not only men and a place to train to the fledgling aviation section of the U.S. Army but also materials. The spruce forest that covered much of the western part of the state supplied excellent building materials for airplanes. President Woodrow Wilson encouraged Boy Scouts to scour the forest for usable trees. A Charlotte newspaper editor was disturbed when twenty men from North Carolina were ordered

These finished airplane propellers were manufactured by Giant Furniture Company in High Point. *State Archives of North Carolina.*

to Washington State to harvest spruce, as there was an overlooked "vast spruce forest on Grandfather Mountain." The spruce trees on neighboring Mount Mitchell and in the Black Mountains were being harvested by the Perley and Crockett Lumber Company under government contract. In High Point, the Giant Furniture Company began producing wooden propellers for the airplanes.[37]

Despite the tragedies of World War I, there were advancements in aviation. Airplanes flew faster, prewar experimental aircraft flew in combat missions as early as 1918, the United States experimented with unpiloted flying bombs and aircraft production boomed.

4

LINDBERGH, RICKENBACKER AND EARHART

THE GOLDEN AGE OF AVIATION

The fairgrounds at Morganton were abuzz with excitement. Henry Westall, the Asheville native and World War I aviator, was bringing an airplane to the town for a combined Fourth of July and welcome home celebration. In the spring of 1919, Westall and leading members of the Asheville community had organized the Asheville Aerial Corporation and purchased a Canuck, the Canadian version of a Curtiss J-N-4 "Jenny." The Jenny was shipped via railroad and arrived on June 11; it was then stored in a hangar at Baird's Bottom on Beaverdam. Westall made his flight over Asheville on June 19. One newspaper reported that fifteen thousand people, from lawns, city streets and rooftops, saw him fly over the city for thirty minutes, reaching "a hundred miles an hour on a boulevard paved with ozone." On July 3, Westall flew from Asheville to Morganton, becoming the first person to fly over the Blue Ridge Mountains. He performed several flights on July 4, carrying passengers. From Morganton, he flew over Hickory, heading toward Winston-Salem, and then to Greensboro and Concord. In August, he flew for three hours from Concord back to Asheville. With no navigational aids or aeronautical maps, pilots often followed railroads (the iron compass) to various towns.[38]

In 1919, aviators made appearances across the state, not only in Morganton but also at points farther east. Aviators were plentiful, as were surplus airplanes. The Gaston County Chamber of Commerce relayed information that the government was selling airplanes. All an interested person had to do was write to the chamber for more information. Aviation

Henry Westall landed in Morganton on Fairground Hill, July 4, 1919. *Burke County Public Library.*

promoters and enthusiasts did not even need to go to Canada, as Westall had done. Most towns and cities held welcome home parades for veterans. New Bern's parade drew fifteen thousand people, with airplanes from Camp Glenn and a fifty-pig barbecue. Fayetteville's parade had a squadron of planes from the just-established Camp Bragg. Wadesboro's celebration boasted not only a plane but a tank as well. In Lumberton, veterans from three different wars walked in the parade while airplanes flew overhead. Two airplanes were involved in the festivities in Rocky Mount. A parade for Black soldiers in Wadesboro also featured an airplane. Lincolnton's parade included not only an airplane but also veterans from the Civil War, Spanish-American War and World War I—as did the parade in Statesville. Governor Thomas Bickett spoke at the celebration in Rockingham, as well as an event at Moore's Creek, both of which included airplanes. Concord's celebration drew ten thousand guests and an army airplane.[39]

To help pay for the war, the Victory Loan of 1919 was launched across the nation. People were encouraged to buy gold notes that would mature in May 1923, at that time earning almost 5 percent interest. While plagued by inferior gasoline, five airplanes visiting Raleigh put on a good show in an effort to encourage people to buy bonds. The planes included one German Fokker and three Curtiss biplanes. One of the Curtiss planes swooped "around tall buildings like an immense bird. One standing at a distance could see the crowd instinctively duck down when the big plane came towards them." More activities and a total of eleven airplanes would have been possible had Raleigh possessed a decent landing field and better gasoline.[40]

There were a couple of other publicity tours launched by the military. The *Black Cat*, an airplane from Langley Field in Virginia, visited several eastern towns, including Tarboro, Greenville, Kinston, Goldsboro and Wilson. Another plane from Langley Field, *Skull and Bones*, visited Durham, Wadesboro, Rockingham, Concord, Salisbury, High Point, Greensboro, Lincolnton, Hamlet, Charlotte and Louisburg. Demonstrations included more than just an airplane that swooped into a local landing field. A Raleigh newspaper reported that there was "Looping, Diving, tail-spinning and doing the Immelmann turn with trimmings." The officers and mechanics with these planes were on recruiting missions, enticing men to not only be aviators but also learn other trades. The pilot of the *Black Cat*, Mooresville native Augustus Leazar, told a reporter that "men who joined the air service have an opportunity to learn forty-eight trades."

The Raleigh business district can be seen in this 1919 aerial image, looking southeast. *Albert Barden Collection, State Archives of North Carolina.*

Enlisted men got a $3,000 education working with the best motors and tool shops that money could buy.[41]

Belvin Maynard was the talk of the state. The North Carolina native and World War I veteran flier broke a world record by doing 318 loops in sixty-seven minutes. Then, in October 1919, he won the longest air race yet held—one thousand miles—from Long Island, New York, to Toronto, Canada, and back. Maynard was back in Raleigh on November 2, 1919, landing his de Havilland biplane that also carried his mechanic William E. Kline and their dog, Trixie. Two days later, he flew out with a passenger: Governor Thomas Bickett. The first North Carolina governor to fly, Bickett was supposed to speak in Wake Forest. On leaving with Maynard, Bickett supposedly said, "Tell Max Gardner [then lieutenant governor] to make a good governor." However, Maynard was not able to find a place to land in Wake Forest and returned to Raleigh, where Bickett sped off in a car to the event. Maynard then flew to Clinton, where twenty-five thousand people had turned out to honor him. On December 5, Maynard flew to Winston-Salem, where the new airfield, off Kernersville Road, was named Maynard Field in his honor.[42]

The 1920s brought a tremendous amount of change to North Carolina. Women gained the right to vote in August 1920; by 1923, North Carolina had overtaken Massachusetts as the leading textile-producing state in the nation; and the state continued to lead the nation in the production of tobacco. Thanks to the work of the "Good Roads Governor," Cameron Morrison, the state's road system was greatly improved. Even the Black business community in Durham was prospering. That's not to say that the prosperity was felt evenly across the state. Despite new schools, the illiteracy rate was high, and many farmers left their farms to seek employment in industries in urban centers.

With the advancements in aviation, the farmers' fields, fairgrounds and golf courses were now too small for airplanes to take off and land. More powerful engines called for bigger planes. And they were beginning to carry more passengers and freight. Some of the larger municipalities, like Winston-Salem, contemplated creating larger airfields. One sought-after opportunity was to become an official U.S. Postal Service stop. Long-distance mail often traveled by railroad. The local postmaster would take the outgoing mail to the train station, where it would be picked up. Incoming mail would then be taken back to the local post office. Airmail offered a speedy alternative for those who needed to get that letter to its destination a little more quickly. On January 2, 1912, there was an exhibition flying event held in Wilmington,

Governor Thomas Bickett (*right*) became the first North Carolina governor to fly. He is pictured here with Belvin Maynard. *State Archives of North Carolina.*

where Lincoln Beachey flew 1,200 postcards around Highwood Park and then landed. The first official letter delivered by airplane was sent to Governor Bickett by the Aero Club of America, arriving on May 16, 1918. While the letter was a congratulatory message on the beginnings of mail service through the air, it would be almost a decade before regular airmail service began in North Carolina.[43]

In December 1918, several newspapers reported that five airplanes, while working on an airmail route from Hampton, Virginia, to Columbia, South Carolina, were spotted in the eastern part of the state. They were using a cultivated field near the state hospital in Raleigh to survey the area between Raleigh, Williamsboro and Pinehurst. Although not official, Pinehurst already had seasonal airmail delivery.

The landing field in Pinehurst, described as being one of the best in the South, was located on the golf course. There was also a proposal for airmail service between Asheville and the resort in Chimney Rock in 1916. Efforts to acquire the government contract to provide a landing field appeared in the news from time to time. Gastonia, Raleigh and Charlotte were mentioned

An airplane is seen at Knollwood Airport in Pinehurst. The plane is emblazoned with "*La Touraine Coffee.*" Two men pose next to the plane with a box of coffee. *Pryor Emerson Humphrey Photograph Collection, State Archives of North Carolina.*

in 1920; Reidsville in 1922; Charlotte again in 1925. But the landing field would not be located in any of these places. Lindley Field in Greensboro became the first official U.S. Post Office airmail stop. Airmail was proposed in Greensboro in 1927, but problems with lighting the field delayed the action, and it was not until May 1, 1928, that the first plane landed. While many locations wanted an airmail stop, many landing fields failed to meet certain requirements. Landing fields had to be lit at night; radio beacons were established to guide pilots; and airplanes had to have radios to receive radio reports. Originally, the U.S. Postal Service had its own pilots. Then in 1926, airmail was delivered via private companies.[44]

The Airmail Act of February 1925, also known as the Kelly Act after its author, Pennsylvania Representative M. Clyde Kelly, allowed small airlines to bid for contracts to carry the mail. Winning bids allowed carriers to be paid based on the weight of the mail carried. The Air Commerce Act of 1926, signed into law by President Calvin Coolidge in May 1926, created the Aeronautic Branch of the Commerce Department. This law developed safety standards, required pilots to be licensed and aircraft to be certified and registered, established national air traffic regulations and encouraged the development of navigational aids. Originally, the federal government was responsible for airport planning and development, but this requirement was removed from the bill. Due to these two acts, along with surplus War World I de Havilland aircraft, the nascent aviation industry in the United States received a boost.[45]

North Carolinians were becoming more cognizant of the need for better landing facilities. The editor of the *Gastonia Gazette* believed that more planes would land in Gastonia but were afraid to attempt "on account of the dangerous nature of the field." State newspapers carried stories of some recent local landings that had resulted in planes having their landing gear disabled. In some locations, it was private individuals who provided better landing fields, and in other locations, municipalities created these spaces. A survey by the Aeronautical Chamber of Commerce listed eighty-seven commercial flying services in the United States, yet North Carolina had next to none, with just one landing field at Camp Bragg and ten emergency fields, such as the racetrack in Goldsboro, the golf course in Pinehurst and the country club in Wilmington.[46]

Greensboro

The promotion of new landing fields came from different directions. Local chambers of commerce played a vital role in some enterprises. In 1923, the Greensboro Chamber of Commerce had a committee to explore the "establishment of an aeroplane landing field." The editor of the *News and Record* was critical, writing that every couple of years, someone suggested an "airplane landing field." A committee was appointed, investigations were conducted and a report was issued, all coming to naught. "It is possible that Greensboro ought to take this business of providing a landing field somewhat more seriously." No progress had been made by the end of 1924, when an editor wrote, "One of the[se] days Greensboro is going to want a landing field." Greensboro did have some sort of field, as in May and June 1925, two different airshows took place. The first utilized a field near or at the fairgrounds, while the second used the Sedgefield Landing Field. Yet that desire to be an official stop on the airmail route was strong. At the chamber office, a yardstick was laid on a map between New York and New Orleans, and Greensboro fell on that line. The chamber brought in an engineer to survey the area and look for a place to establish a landing field "which could be acceptable to the United States government for mail service." The field

This page: Gene Brown, the Eastern Airline pilot who flew the first airmail into the state, took time to sign a couple of photographs when he visited Lindley Field. *Author's collection.*

had to be 1,000 feet wide and 3,000 feet long, level and without obstructions, with "hangars, fueling devises, repair shops, and lighting for night services." The Greensboro committee invited interested parties from Winston-Salem and High Point to partner with them. Just over 112 acres were purchased from the Lindley family in Guilford County. With twelve thousand people in attendance, Lindley Field opened in May 1927. Officials from Pitcairn Aviation, which had the government contract, were on hand. The City of Greensboro leased the field for one dollar a year and began making improvements. The grass field was put in better shape, and a passenger terminal and hangar were constructed, along with a radio beacon. An official weather station was also activated. On November 6, 1930, passenger service began. Dixie Flying Service transported a load of passengers from Greensboro to Washington, D.C. More land was purchased by 1935, but shortly thereafter, the airfield was closed for repairs. The county assumed ownership once again, freeing up funds for Works Progress Administration improvements. The runways were paved, and the Greensboro–High Point Airport Authority assumed control in 1942.[47]

Charlotte

Charlotte was likewise in play, but its road to having an airfield was not as easy as Greensboro's. It's possible the first flight in the Queen City took place in May 1910, when Charles K. Hamilton, the "Crazy Man of the Air," flew at the fairgrounds. There was even a discussion of establishing a Curtiss or Wright aviation school in the city later that year but before the air meet. Almost a decade later, Henry Westall talked with the chamber of commerce about establishing a landing field and starting a commercial air service to carry passengers. When an aviator planning a cross-country trip in 1919 sent the chamber a letter to ask where he might land to secure supplies, the chamber selected the "old athletic field" at Camp Greene and marked it with a large white cross made of canvas. In February 1920, the Charlotte Aero Club was organized. The leaders of the club, Charles E. Lambeth, Mebane Long and Don R. Harris, were all former military aviators. The club was to encourage "any legitimate movement that will have for its aim the putting of Charlotte on the map as one of the cities of the United States that is alive to the possibilities of commercial aviation." They wanted to "find suitable landing fields for passing aviators." Belvin Maynard spoke in February 1921 at lunch time for the Aero Club, and he spoke later that evening to the Junior Order of United American Mechanics. The Charlotte Aero Club seems to disappear between 1922 and 1929, when a new Charlotte Aero Club was incorporated, with William C. Osborne, John J. Weeks, W. Fitts and Neswmith Thompson listed as stockholders.[48]

In the fall of 1919, the *Charlotte Observer* secured some biplanes for promotional purposes. At least once referred to as the "Charlotte Observer's Aerial Circus," the planes flew over the town of Davidson and then Concord and Kannapolis. Over the latter two towns, the plane, piloted by L.E. Shealy, scattered "copies of a special Concord-Kannapolis edition of the paper." Two other pilots were J.W. Ironmonger and Scotty Campbell. The planes were based in Myers Park, and the whole affair seems to have been a short-lived publicity stunt.[49]

While airplanes seemed to be landing at various places across Charlotte, it was evident that a dedicated landing field was needed. H.L. Morrow, a representative of the Curtiss Aeroplane and Motor Company, which was attempting to set up a route between Asheville and Pinehurst, told a local newspaper that to be a progressive city, Charlotte needed a permanent landing field. "The day of aerial transportation for business purposes has arrived," Morrow said. Plus, the government was working to establish an airmail route between Washington, D.C., and Atlanta, with "Charlotte as one of the stops en route."[50]

Despite not having an airfield up to grade, per government standards, Charlotte still had pilots flying there. Osmond Barringer leased enough land at the old Camp Greene to set up the Barringer Landing Field. There, he worked with the Southern Aeroplane Company, which brought in a French Farman biplane and began offering rides. In June 1920, it was reported that the landing field was being graded, with the addition of hangars and a clubhouse. Myers Park landing field was also still in use. By early 1922, only the Myers Park field appeared to be in operation, as one visiting military aviator stated that the Camp Greene site was excellent and only needed the city to take action. There was some discussion about building a landing field at Sherwood Forest in 1924, a site that could "accommodate hundreds of planes." Yet no action was taken. The polo field at Myers Park was reported as being "almost impossible for larger planes to land," although smaller planes frequently used the field. However, by March 1927, "advancement" had eliminated the Myers Park landing field.[51]

In the summer of 1926, the subject of an airmail stop in Charlotte came up again. This time, the proposed landing field was the infield of the recently opened Charlotte Speedway in Pineville. That speedway closed in 1927, and there is no indication that it was ever used for a landing field. Discussion of acquiring a new, larger landing field heated up as airmail routes were discussed. R.H. Horton, an investigator for the department of commerce, visited the city in 1926, a visit that led the chamber of commerce to begin discussions with the city commissioners. E.C. Griffith and S.B. Alexander, owners of the old Camp Greene site, offered to sell their property for the landing field. Charlotte sent a delegation to Washington, D.C., in February 1927 to meet with officials to discuss the possibility of the Queen City getting on the airmail route, while it was announced that an option was secured on a track of land owned by C.F. Dalton and Charles Alexander on Statesville Road. Nothing seems to have materialized from these early efforts to produce a better landing field in Charlotte. Even Charles Lindbergh's 1927 visit to North Carolina, along with a proposed visit by the Pan American Good Will Fliers, could not galvanize city officials to take action. "Charlotte cannot afford to again be caught without such a landing field," cried the editor of the *Charlotte News*. "This city has delayed long enough. Raleigh has acted. Winston-Salem is building. Asheville is considering a special election to vote bonds for an airport. Charlotte has both the funds for such a step and the time for dilatory tactics has passed."[52]

In April 1928, the chamber of commerce purchased 215 acres of land west of the old Camp Greene site. That same month, it was announced that United Airways of North Carolina Inc. was opening a commercial airport to the north of Charlotte on the North Tryon Street Extension and Derita Road. The airport near the Camp Greene site was named the Charlotte Airport. Engineers were called in to properly lay out the two 2,500-foot-long runways, and the roof of the Charlotte Supply Company on South Mint Street was painted with letters twelve feet high to mark the airport. By June, aviators were already making use of the site, although grading work was not complete. In October, a trimotor Ford arrived and began giving sightseeing

A postcard shows the Municipal Airport in Charlotte with its WPA-era hangar. *Author's collection.*

tours, prompting the editor of the *Charlotte Sunday Observer* to lead off with the headline "Feverish Activity at Charlotte Airport." By the end of the year, several other planes had arrived to give passengers rides or perform stunts. One of the pilots was nineteen-year-old Gladys Poole, who "amazed the gaping multitude with some of the most sensational stunt flying ever witnessed at the Charlotte Airport." For the first recorded time, Santa Claus landed at the Charlotte Airport on November 30, 1928. Airmail officially arrived at the Charlotte Airport on April 1, 1930. Approximately twenty-five thousand pieces of mail awaited the two planes, one of which was coming from the south and the other coming from the north. While each plane was on the ground for only five minutes, the Eastern Air Transport Inc. pilots received numerous gifts, as arranged by the chamber of commerce.[53]

Winston-Salem

Over six thousand people witnessed Lincoln Beachey fly in Winston-Salem in early April 1911. And less than a year later, John Lehman and W.H. Sloan organized the Winston-Salem Aerial Company. Their plan was to build two-passenger airships based on a Curtiss biplane. They built a model that was exhibited in March 1912, but like it did for most of the early aerial companies, news of the venture quickly disappeared from the press. Local residents were preparing for a visit by the *Skull and Bones* aircraft in 1919 and secured the farm of W.N. Reynolds. The alfalfa field was mowed, and the Curtiss JN-4H delighted several thousand spectators. Several other planes visited the Reynolds Landing Strip over the next few weeks. One editor believed that if Winston-Salem could build a hangar, stockpile supplies and hire a mechanic, the city could lead the area in aviation. W.N. Reynolds told the city the second week of July 1919 that the field was reverting to a hay field. Officials began looking for another landing field. By October, another location had been selected, this time managed by the Winston-Salem Aviation Company. This became Maynard Field. Later, Winston-Salem partnered with Greensboro and High Point to open the Friendship Airport. This field proved beneficial for Greensboro, but it was not convenient to Winston-Salem, and the city began looking for another option. Miller Airport was graded and put into service in October 1927. On the day the airport was dedicated, Robert Laster purchased the field and then gave it to the county, which then transferred it to the airport commission. R.J. Reynolds Jr. brought a division of his Reynolds Aviation to Miller Field. Reynolds Aviation provided passenger

The aircraft of Gates Flying Service in Winston-Salem, circa 1925. *The Clyde Pangborn Collection, The Museum of Flight.*

service to New York, Detroit, Baltimore, Philadelphia and, on the weekends, Myrtle Beach and Wrightsville Beach. The company was disbanded, and Camel City Flying Service set up shop at Miller Field in 1932. The new company offered pilot training, charter flights and hangar storage and sold Piper and Stinson airplanes. As a part of the New Deal, the Civil Works Administration extended runways, improved the hangars and upgraded the lighting system. In 1938, additional property was purchased, and a fourth runway was built. Eastern Air Lines began serving the airport in 1940, and in 1942, Miller Field was renamed Smith Reynolds Airport.[54]

Asheville

It was a much smaller crowd, estimated at 1,200 people, that witnessed Lincoln Beachey make a short flight from the Baird's Bottom Landing Field in Asheville in 1911. His plane was shipped in on the railroad, and reportedly, after a few minutes in the air, he stated that the mountain air currents were "too tricky for him and abandoned the idea of any further flying." While local aviator Henry K. Crowell was in Asheville just two years later, trying to woo city leaders to establish an aviation training station, it was not until May 1919 that the Asheville Aero Company, with L.L. Jenkins as president, was organized. This is the company for which Henry Westall flew. The *Asheville Times* had an airplane, the *City of Asheville*, stationed at the field for a time. Another field in use by 1920 was located near the Biltmore Estate. Belvin Maynard landed there in April 1920 before he was whisked off to speak to the Rotary Club. The Baird's Bottom site was declared too small, and in 1923, it was flooded to create Beaver Lake. In 1920, Scott Dillingham established Dillingham Landing Field between Asheville and Oteen. About the same time, a landing strip in the Emma community, just west of Asheville, opened. It was on this field that test pilot Harry Brooks, while attempting to fly a Ford Flivver from Michigan to Florida, was forced to land. This landing field was also known as the Josephson Airport and the Asheville Airpark. In 1930, Carrier Field, an old horse racetrack on the banks of the French Broad River, was converted into an airstrip. The formal opening included stunt flying and parachute jumping, and eventually, the field had hangars for storing airplanes. This landing field was later renamed Owen Field in honor of local aviator Dr. James E. Owen.[55]

There was a push for a larger commercial airport starting in 1925, with a survey of sites held in February 1927. The site selected was in Fletcher. Talks were still ongoing well over a year later, and it was not until August 23, 1929, that the Asheville-Hendersonville Airport opened. A three-day "aerial derby" was held, with appearances by speed record-holder Douglas Davis, stunt woman and parachutist Miss Mabel Cody (the niece of Buffalo Bill) and parachute altitude record holder Jack McCullum. An estimated crowd of ten thousand gathered to see the aerobatics, with several hundred spectators taking a ride over Cane Creek Valley. Having outgrown this site, the airport purchased a new site of 123 acres in 1936. The new Asheville-Hendersonville Airport was partially a WPA project, with at least $100,000 coming through the program. However, in August 1936, construction halted for a time. There were charges that "faulty materials" were used to pave the runways. New plans were drawn up and submitted to the WPA in September. In December, the WPA proposed cutting $40,000 from the project, money it said it no longer had. The project was back on track by the late spring of 1937, this time at a cost of $150,000. Airmail service, conducted by Eastern Air Lines, began that October.[56]

Raleigh

Back in 1910, Raleigh hosted the second aviation meet in the state. Seeing an airplane fly at the state fair became a common spectacle. As they did in many other places, bigger and faster airplanes outgrew those sites. Finding an adequate site in Raleigh became a challenge, just as it was in other cities across the state. For a time, the airplanes used a field next to the state hospital. There is also a reference to airplanes landing at the state fairgrounds/Camp Polk in 1919. In January 1919, there was discussion of establishing a "large aviation landing field with suitable hangars, sleeping quarters and proper markers." A field east of Raleigh was designated in May 1919. This might have been a site not far from the Old Confederate Soldiers' Home on New Bern Avenue. An airshow took place there in October 1919, with aerialists wing walking and hanging from their planes' landing gear. Yet the need for a better landing field persisted. When one or two planes came in, it was no problem on the existing field. "But in a few years when they are dropping down like automobiles along every street

Roscoe Turner's barnstorming plane *Cloudland Express* is pictured in Raleigh in 1921. Turner is on the wing next to the pilot's seat beside his copilot. Al Runser and Carr Booker are standing to the left. *State Archives of North Carolina.*

in the city, a little field would be no more use for the city's requirements than two hundred feet in front of the Yarborough House." When a new Curtiss Oriole ran off the small field and into a ditch, local pilot Roscoe Turner told the newspaper, "A $10,000 plane smashed up, all for the want of a suitable landing field." Turner hoped that the crack-up would "spur Raleigh to greater efforts to fit up a suitable field."[57]

For three years, Raleigh was without a landing field. This changed in January 1924, when a field was secured off Garner Road, two miles from the city. The grass landing strip was 1,500 feet in length, and the Dixie Oil Company supplied gasoline and oil. Yet in 1926, there were cries that the Garner Road landing strip was lacking, and a new site near the state farm was proposed. A survey at the end of the year selected a new site off Tryon Road. There were names floated for the new airport, including the Lindbergh Airport; Robbins Field, after a World War I aviator killed in France; and the Capital City Airport. The landing field would eventually become known as the Marshburn-Robbins Landing Field, or simply as the Municipal Field. Governor Angus McLean was one of the featured speakers when the airport officially opened in September 1927. Less than a year later, a second airfield opened in Raleigh, possibly at the old site on Garner Road. This landing field was known as Poindexter Field, after H.B. Poindexter. The new aviation company that ran service in one two-passenger plane was known as Carolina Airlines, incorporated by Alton Stewart, Eugene Mills and L.R. Fisher.[58]

When Poindexter Field opened in January 1928, the *News and Observer* declared that an "Air War Looms in Capital City." The Mashburn-Robbins Field experimented with lights for night landings in March 1928; new signs, with fifteen-foot-long arrows, were installed that spring to help aviators find the field; a sister ship to the *Spirit of St. Louis* was at the airport in October. Over at Poindexter Field, legendary actor Will Rogers landed in March 1928; the area's first parachute jump from an airplane took place in April 1928 in front of a crowd of fifteen thousand; and Smith Reynolds set down his Waco 10 in June.[59]

With two fields, the battle for the position as Raleigh's official airport was not over. Neither field seemed adequate to serve the state capital. Then in April 1929, it was announced that the Curtiss Airport and Aviation School, which operated several other airports, was looking at a three-hundred-acre farm three miles south of the city. H.B. Poindexter was in charge of the new field, which included hangars and lights. The Curtiss Corporation flew in four brand-new aircraft, which were stored at Poindexter Field while

Eastern Air Lines flew the Great Silver Fleet into Raleigh and other cities in the 1930s. *Author's collection.*

construction and grading was underway. The airport went by the name Curtiss Field, Curtiss-White Airport, the Raleigh Airport and, eventually, the Raleigh Municipal Airport. By June, pilots were landing at the field, although it was not quite complete. In September, passenger service began, with Eastern Air Lines arriving. A Bellanca monoplane was christened the *City of Raleigh* by Miss Annie Laurie Underwood, "Raleigh's first woman flier," while former Secretary of the Navy Josephus Daniels welcomed officers from the airline. Poindexter Field was converted into a gun range by September 1929. The Mashburn-Robbins Field quickly disappeared from the records, leaving Raleigh with only one "municipal airport."[60]

The Raleigh Municipal Airport served the area for decades. Amelia Earhart flew an Autogiro into the airport in November 1931. She told a group gathered at a luncheon, "Flying is being made safer every day....In the near future I believe that any city without an airport will face economic loss." The airport closed for a brief time in in early 1934. With help from the WPA, the airport reopened in September 1934 with passenger and airmail service. The special speakers that day were Captain Eddie Rickenbacker and Governor John C.B. Ehringhaus. With fifty-three planes on hand, it was proclaimed the largest gathering of aircraft in state history. After World War II, commercial flights were moved to the new Raleigh-Durham Airport. Small local planes were stationed at the airport until 1973, when the facility was closed.[61]

A crowd gathers at the Raleigh Municipal Airport, circa 1935. *Albert Barden Collection, State Archives of North Carolina.*

The *City of Raleigh* was christened by Annie Underwood. *State Archives of North Carolina.*

Wilmington

Following Lincoln Beachey's flight from Wilmington in 1911, there seemed to always be some airplane or hydroplane passing overhead or landing nearby. The Audubon Field was mentioned as a site of frequent landings and improvements starting in 1919. *Wilmington Morning Star* editor Ben McNeill got a chance to take a ride with an aviator from Pope Field who had landed at the Audubon Field. Prior to his maiden flight, McNeill was spotted sucking on a lemon "to guard against possible seasickness or cloudsickness, and chewing on a cigar" at the same time. Soon, the engine roared to life, and the Curtiss took to the air. At six hundred feet, "automobiles that had brought spectators were crawling away like ants….The Earth continued to drop away, and to spread out in an ever-widening pattern." As McNeill climbed higher, what appeared to be toy ships floated in the Cape Fear River, the "whole world was smooth and green. Trees looked like grass, and roads were white threads stretched along the green." It was here that McNeill's "knees felt useless, and his midriff heaved," although the pilot did not seem to notice. At least twice, the pilot shut off the engine to talk with McNeill. The second time, the pilot put the plane into a nosedive, in which McNeill thought he was going to die. After a few more maneuvers, they landed without incident. To assure those on the ground that he was safe—and maybe to convince himself—McNeill "asked for a cigarette, in what he thought was a mild conservational voice. Instead, he screamed, for indeed he was quite deaf," thanks to the roar of the engine.[62]

While there were discussions about a new field, the Audubon site continued in service. The military used the site frequently. When planes from Charleston arrived to observe target practice at Fort Caswell, they used Audubon Field. In 1922, the local branch of the Texas Oil Company was awarded a contract to furnish oil and gas for all naval airplanes that landed at the field. There were other sites in the greater Wilmington area also being used. Wrightsville Beach was being considered for a government landing field as early as 1922; Southport frequently had seaplanes land and tie up at the docks; three airplanes from the Twenty-Second Aero Squadron used Carolina Beach for ten days in 1922. The discussion of a new airport led the county to construct a landing field near Gordon Road. Originally, the landing field had two runways. The new landing field formally opened on Memorial Day 1928 and was named Bluethenthal Field, in honor of the local aviator Arthur Bluethenthal, who was killed during World War I. Despite the work, the new field did pose problems. In October 1928, Kentucky Lieutenant

Bluethenthal Airport was dedicated in May 1928, with J.O. Carr delivering the address. *Cape Fear Museum of History and Science.*

Governor A.D. Breathitt, who was on the presidential campaign trail for Al Smith, Governor of New York, crashed into a log upon takeoff. Breathitt and his pilot were uninjured, but the lieutenant governor was forced to take a car to his next appointment.[63]

Much of the hubbub about new and improved landing fields did more than simply help local aviators or businesses. A certain crop of adventurers fueled the need for bigger and better landing fields. Part of the desire for a new landing field in Raleigh in 1926 was the hope that famed polar explorer Richard Byrd would visit as he traveled around the country. Then Charles Lindbergh, the most famous person in the world after his May 1927 solo flight from New York to Paris, went on tour in the United States after the event. In three months, he and his plane, *The Spirit of St. Louis*, visited forty-eight states. While in North Carolina in October, Lindbergh flew over Salisbury and Lexington to drop messages. *The Spirit of St. Louis* touched down in Winston-Salem and Greensboro. In Greensboro, the crowds swelled to fifty thousand. Governor McLean proclaimed Lindbergh to be the "greatest hero of the present day." In Winston-Salem, with fifteen thousand schoolchildren looking on, he spoke at Miller Field for just over six minutes on the importance of aviation and the development of commercial aviation. Many newspapers in the state were quick to point out that North Carolina native William A. Winston was the man who taught Lindbergh to fly. After spending the night at the Robert E. Lee Hotel, "Lucky Lindy" was on his way to Danville. Entertainer, actor and writer Will Rogers visited Raleigh in October 1932 on his return from his journey through Central and South America. When the Raleigh Municipal Airport was reopened in 1934, Eddie Rickenbacker was on hand. At the luncheon held on dedication day, Rickenbacker was given a "standing ovation as America's leading ace during" World War I. Amelia Earhart visited the state at least twice. She was in Kitty Hawk in 1928, when the cornerstone of the Wright Brothers

Monument was laid. Earhart returned in November 1931 to visit the Raleigh Municipal Airport, where she spoke and christened a new airplane. Flying an Autogiro with Beech-Nut Chewing Gum as a sponsor, she also visited Fayetteville, Southern Pines and Charlotte. Military aviator James Doolittle visited the Knollwood Airport in 1930 and proclaimed the grass runway to be one of the best around.[64]

Various aircraft and pilots across the state created some legal trouble. Harry Runsur was charged with trespassing and was fined fifty dollars for landing in the field of W.S. Murchison in October 1919. Pilot Earl S. Orr was in Raleigh when an arrest warrant arrived. His crime? Disturbing the peace on a Sunday in his airplane while advertising for cigarettes. Several were arrested at the airport in Winston-Salem in 1925, charged with flying narcotics from Maryland into the area. Calvary Episcopal Church near the Asheville-Hendersonville Airport in Fletcher took out an insurance policy in case an airplane crashed into the church building while taking off or landing. An airplane that was giving a demonstration on a Sunday in Hoke County raised the ire of one local who believed, "If other work is a violation of the law of the Sabbath, such entertainment should be prevented by officers. The owners of the airplane gave parachute leaps and took people to ride.

Will Rogers is greeted by Mrs. Josephus Daniels at the airport in Raleigh in October 1932. *State Archives of North Carolina.*

Amelia Earhart, flying an Autogiro, visited Pinehurst on November 11, 1931. *State Archives of North Carolina.*

Got some money out of it, likely." This was a concern in other counties as well. In Charlotte, local ministers tried to work with city leaders and got flying banned between 9:00 a.m. and 12:30 p.m. on Sundays. The sheriff of Buncombe County, while flying to Salisbury, used the opportunity to look for moonshine stills. He spotted five in Buncombe, three in McDowell and two in Rutherford County. An airplane was used in a 1937 manhunt after seven prisoners from the Caledonia Prison in Halifax County escaped and commandeered a car. The car was later found abandoned in High Point.[65]

A curious case involved Frank Elmore. As the story goes, Elmore grew up in Georgia and flew for a while with Asheville Police Sergeant Frank Messer, possibly for the U.S. Navy. At one point, Elmore was flying out of the Asheville-Hendersonville Airport until he absconded with his employer's airplane. He was arrested for violating the National Motor Vehicle Act, but the courts ruled that it did not apply to airplanes. Elmore then flew the mail from Atlanta to Miami and later joined the Cuban revolutionaries, becoming the "ace of the rebel air force." He also allegedly smuggled guns from the ROTC armory at the University of Georgia. Later, Elmore was arrested for robbing a bank in Dublin, Georgia. He was sentenced to ten years on the chain gang for both the bank robbery and gun running. After escaping, he returned to North Carolina to visit his wife in Hendersonville and was arrested in Bat Cave in October 1934.[66]

In 1929, the North Carolina General Assembly passed several acts regulating aviation. It defined terms like *aeronautics*, *instructor*, *aircraft*, *airman*, *navigation* and *navigation facility*, *airports*, *airport hazards*, *air school*, *flying clubs*, *navigable air space*, *public aircraft* and *restricted area*. Cities, towns and counties were authorized to establish airports; they could acquire property for airports through purchase and eminent domain; and public owners of airports could charge fees for the use of these airports and adopt regulations regarding their use. Pilots had permission to fly aircraft over the state, except at a dangerously low altitude. Pilots performing acrobatics over a "thickly inhabited area" could be charged with a class 1 misdemeanor. Pilots also needed federally issued licenses. Aircraft had to be airworthy and registered. Stealing an airplane was a felony, while tampering with an aircraft or flying while impaired were misdemeanors.[67]

Airplanes were used in countless ways. When World War I aviator William D. Robbins was reinterred in Oakwood Cemetery in Raleigh in 1921, an airplane flew overhead and dropped red, white and blue flowers while the service was conducted. During the November 1929 football game between the University of Virginia and the University of North Carolina, several people flew into Chapel Hill for the game, including Virginia's Governor Harry F. Byrd. As 270 men toiled in a remote section of Hyde County on a Works Progress Administration project, an airplane brought fresh food, paychecks and medical supplies to the site. In 1939, part of the cast for *The Lost Colony*, a play performed on Roanoke Island that depicts the arrival of English settlers, arrived by plane.[68]

Airplanes were also used for various campaigns and promotional ventures. When Needham L. Broughton ran for the North Carolina House of Representatives, he had campaign literature dropped from an airplane in Stanly County. A Fokker monoplane performed a broadcasting test in 1927 over Winston-Salem, sending out a message that could be heard without "artificial receivers." Around the holidays in 1927, flying salesman Dallas M. Speer of the Curtiss Candy Corporation flew over Raleigh to drop candy with little parachutes attached. At the Asheville-Hendersonville Airport in 1930, a flock of guineas was released. Anyone who caught one of those guineas got a free ride. A plane that flew over the Locust community in Stanly County dropped advertisements for the

The first passenger plane left Greensboro on November 6, 1930. *Charles A. Farrell Photograph Collection, State Archives of North Carolina.*

Robbins Flying Service. C.J. Emons had tickets dropped on Pinehurst, with special offers on merchandise and a few free airplane rides. Likewise, in Watauga County in 1931, select newspapers were dropped out of an airplane with free tickets for rides. In Wadesboro, an airplane was hired to drop circulars regarding an upcoming land sale.[69]

Some veterans of previous engagements were anxious for rides. George W. Finch, a Confederate veteran from Nash County, took his first ride at the age of seventy-eight. He stated that he "had never expected to take such a ride in the sky but this being his first opportunity, he seized the chance and enjoyed the ride very much." The old soldiers at the United Confederate Veterans Reunion in Charlotte in June 1929 were treated to rides. Often, the 1,200 Boy Scouts responsible for escorting the veterans around got to fly as well.[70]

Fighting the dreaded boll weevil, a pest that destroys cotton plants, was a job for airplanes. But regional farmers needed to be convinced that the expense was worth it. Demonstrations on crop-dusting were held in Scotland Neck, Mt. Olive and Rockingham in 1925.[71]

Airplanes were useful for scouting locations for new lakes and for photographing disasters, like the Carolina Coal Mine accident in Sanford in 1925. After the images were developed, they were flown from Pope Field to Washington, D.C. An airplane was used by Carolina Power and Light to survey a fifty-mile stretch of poles from Laurinburg to Hartsville, as they were inaccessible due to standing water. When the chief of police was shot and killed in March 1929, military pilots from Pope Field were asked to provide aerial reconnaissance in seeking the alleged killer. In 1935, airplanes from the Asheville-Hendersonville Airport were used by the Tennessee Valley Authority to survey the land that became the Blue Ridge Parkway.[72]

Airplanes were even being used in the medical field. A doctor from Tarboro flew into Raleigh with $125,000 worth of radium to treat a patient. When a Civilian Conservation Corps worker was injured at the Buxton Camp, an airplane transported him to a hospital in Norfolk. By 1939, L.M. McEwen and Carl McEwen were operating the only air ambulance in the Southeast. Their base was located in Charlotte.[73]

Even the military used the airspace in North Carolina for testing. Following World War I, Brigadier General Billy Mitchell advocated using derelict naval vessels for bombing and destruction by airplanes. To say that military leadership was skeptical would be an understatement. Many believed the airplane would be no match for the firepower of naval vessels.

A biplane dusts an unidentified field in North Carolina. *State Archives of North Carolina.*

Mitchell provided a series of tests. The first occurred off the coast of Virginia in July 1921, when the captured German battleship *Ostfriesland* was sunk by an aerial bombardment. The 1890s battleship USS *Alabama* was targeted in September and was also sent to the bottom of the Chesapeake Bay. In 1923, the tests were moved to North Carolina. An airbase was set up on Cape Hatteras. The USS *New Jersey* and USS *Virginia* were towed near the Diamond Shoals Lighthouse off Cape Hatteras. On September 5, the bombers attacked the two battleships. The *Virginia* sank within thirty minutes. While several bombs missed the *New Jersey*, one 1,100-pound bomb struck the ship, and it rolled over before the pilot could come around for a second attack. Mitchell asserted, "The problem of the destruction of seacraft by Air Forces has been solved and is finished." Few North Carolina newspapers reported on the events. Raleigh's *The News and Observer* had an article, "Ships Sunk Off Cape Hatteras," buried on page five. While Mitchell ran afoul of his superiors, accusing them for an "almost treasonable administration of the national defense" when they invested in battleships instead of aircraft, which resulted in his court-martial, he is considered the father of the U.S. Air Force.[74]

Mitchell's advocacy of air power is well documented. There was another event near Albemarle in December 1927. A recently built concrete bridge over the Pee Dee River was scheduled to be inundated with water once a nearby hydroelectric dam was completed. The first two days of bombing practice were performed with bombs loaded with sand as the bombers flew in different formations and at varied altitudes. The bombers switched to 600-pound and 1,100-pound bombs next. The former did little damage, but the latter demolished the bridge. A couple of months later, the film strip of the events, produced by the army, was shown in Albemarle. Some considered the event "second in importance only to the battleship bombing in 1921," as it showed how "bombs of different weights affected reinforced concrete."[75]

The economic collapse that started in 1929 was just as hard for the airports as it was for other entities. For example, in 1931, the Charlotte Airport was in dire straits and was faced with the possibility of closing. There was a cry to have the city purchase the airport. Yet the city had its own problems and was even discussing floating a bond issue to pay schoolteacher salaries. The acquisition of the airport by the city was put to a special vote. New management arrived at the airport in March 1932, which brought some stability. Statewide, hundreds of banks closed, and many people lost their homes and businesses. The state budget was reduced by one-third. Likewise, the funding of counties and municipalities also

Pope Field at Fort Bragg often sent military airplanes to various airshows and festivals in eastern North Carolina. *Author's collection.*

declined. There was less money for airport investments and improvements. In Greensboro, the county used convicts to grade the municipal airport and repair the drainage ditches. At the Knollwood Airport, fifteen men were put to work on airport improvements.[76]

When Franklin D. Roosevelt became president in March 1933, he implemented the New Deal, a series of programs that sought to bring economic relief. Between July 1933 and March 1939, various public work programs funded tens of thousands of projects across the nation. Every county in the nation benefited from various projects. At first, the program fell under the jurisdiction of the Civil Works Administration. In Winston-Salem, 225 men were hired to improve Miller Municipal Airport. In Salisbury, 160 men were approved to work on that town's local airport. Other towns sought support elsewhere, like Lenoir, which pursued a grant of $7,805 to lease eighty acres of land and construct a two-thousand-foot-long runway near the golf course. Statesville tried to purchase forty to fifty acres for an airport. If the municipality owned the property, then the CWA provided the funds for improvements. The project employed 43 men for forty days. The Charlotte Airport sought $150,000 for improvements. In Durham, CWA funds were used to hire 4 engineers to survey proposed airport sites. Bluethenthal Airport was able to hire 100 local Wilmington men who cleared land and upgraded lighting.[77]

The Civil Works Administration lasted only five months. The Public Works Administration (PWA) came next, along with the Works Progress Administration (WPA). With federal funding available, many localities that wanted an airport or landing field but did not have the means were interested in securing funds. Gibsonville, near Burlington, sought funds to develop an airport on one hundred–plus acres it was considering leasing. When the grant was approved for Huntersville, a fifty-acre track was developed as an airfield. Local citizens were on board with the project and donated poles for electric lines and shrubbery for landscaping at the hangar and on the boundary. These projects lasted for years. The Asheville-Hendersonville Airport, Pitt-Greeneville Airport, Charlotte Airport, Raleigh Municipal Airport and many others all received some type of federal funding prior to the advent of World War II. The WPA even provided funds for thirty-seven towns to mark their closest airports and landing fields with fifteen-foot-tall letters and arrows.[78]

Despite the foreboding economic outlook, the influx of federal dollars allowed work to continue on various projects that had been started in North Carolina. On July 4, 1929, the new Curtiss Field opened three miles south of Raleigh. Within a few days, a monoplane from the Curtiss Flying Service took passengers to Wilmington for a weekend at Wrightsville Beach. Formal passenger service provided by Eastern Air Express began on September 18. Two months later, Underwood bested other students at a contest at Curtiss Field, in which pilots, at a predetermined mark, cut their engines and glided in for a landing. With more than one landing field in Raleigh, there was discussion about which field the city would support.[79]

While the ever-popular airshows slowed during the Great Depression years, they never quite stopped. An airshow with three airplanes in Albemarle in July 1930 brought in several thousand sightseers. In Raleigh that year, at the Curtiss-Wright Airport, "a big air program" was advertised for July Fourth, with "parachute jumping, balloon busting, and dead-stick landing[s]." Boonie Rowe, a former member of the Mabel Cody Flying Circus, made parachute jumps in Shelby and Asheville later that summer. An estimated three thousand attendees came to the Asheville show. Advertised was E.J. Buyck, who was supposed to take an airplane up and then disable it and parachute to safety. Where the airplane was supposed to crash-land was not disclosed. Luckily for those in the surrounding communities, the airplane had engine trouble, and the exhibition was canceled. Demonstration flying was a part of the Mebane Fair in September 1931, and two months later, the *Winnie Mae*, a Lockheed Vega that Wiley

Charlotte Ryland, a Virginia sponsor of the 1941 Rhododendron Festival, disembarks from a Pennsylvania-Central Airlines plane at the Asheville-Hendersonville Airport. *Buncombe County Special Collections, Pack Memorial Public Library.*

Post and Harold Gatty had flown around the world in eight days, toured the state, with stops in Charlotte, Winston-Salem, Goldsboro, Lumberton, Salisbury and Asheville. In most cases, the plane was placed in a hangar, and people were charged a small admission price to see it while Post and Gatty were wined and dined and gave speeches about the importance of aviation and their around-the-world experience.[80]

R.C. King, seen just below the biplane, made his first parachute jump near Greensboro in November 1930. *Author's collection.*

"Dare Devil Jimmy Darby" visited Riverside Field near Elkin in the spring of 1932. In Shelby, the new airfield on the L.A. Jackson farm was opened with a parachute jump by a "one-armed...daredevil." Shelby also hosted Otto Comp, a German aviator who supposably flew with the Red Baron's Flying Circus. Comp lived in Charlotte for a time and then managed the Asheville-Hendersonville Airport in 1930. The American Legion sponsored an airshow at the new Cherryville Airport in October 1933. "Famous Negro Aviator, Lt. Hubert Julian" visited the state in late 1933. Known as "The Black Eagle of Harlem" or the "Negro Lindbergh," the Trinidad native spoke in Durham and flew into Chapel Hill. "Duke Fernald's Daredevil Aces," with Johnny Crowell, flew into Asheville-Hendersonville in 1935. Crowell flew "with his hands tied securely at arm's length over his head." Also on the bill were other fliers who presented "Balloon Busting, Air Races, Serpentine Cutting, [and] Bombing car," as well as "Donnie Marshall, America's champion Bat Wing Parachute Jumper." A show in Goldsboro promised seventy-five airplanes, two hundred pilots and a meeting of the Ninety-Nines, an organization of women pilots.[81]

In August 1938, President Roosevelt signed the Civil Aeronautics Act into law. This new law gave the federal government the power to regulate routes, pricing and safety standards of airlines. Tensions were brewing across

To commemorate the arrival of airmail, the U.S. Postal Service issued special first-day covers for Raleigh (*top*) and Charlotte (*bottom*). *Author's collection.*

Europe, and many were concerned about the unpreparedness of the United States. A couple of months later, an experimental Civilian Pilot Training Program began at thirteen colleges. The program would help the fledgling aviation industry and create a base of reserve pilots with some knowledge. North Carolina State College of Agriculture and Engineering in Raleigh was one of those colleges.

With the success of the program, Roosevelt signed the Civilian Pilot Training Act into law the next year. Inexpensive training was now open to men, women and Black Americans. Over four hundred thousand people were trained across the United States over the next five years. The program connected a local college with a nearby airstrip. Students had to complete seventy-two hours of ground school and a minimum of thirty-five hours of flight instruction. The Civilian Aeronautics Authority (CAA) administered the program, which would also eventually have a smaller, noncollege track. Students were charged $40 for the program, while the CAA paid the schools $20 for the ground school and up to $290 for the flight course. "For every nine boys, there had to be a girl," recalled Kate Adams. So, she and a friend, Jane Winters, "were happy to fill those roles." They attended classes on the campus of North Carolina State College but had to drive to the other side of Raleigh for flight instruction.[82]

There was stiff competition among various communities to get one of the training schools and the accompanying federal dollars. Congressman Zebulon Weaver presented a petition to the secretary of war in June 1940 asking that the Asheville-Hendersonville Airport be considered for one of the schools. Likewise, citizens asked their congressional representative to push Knollwood Airport in Moore County as a place to train pilots. Harold

Cannon Airport was just one of five airports in the greater Charlotte area at the end of the 1930s. *Author's Collection.*

Bachman, with two airplanes and in charge of the field, could handle ten students. The Asheville-Hendersonville Airport was training students by October 1940. Ground classes were held at sites across the state: Brevard College, Catawba College, Cherokee Indian Normal School in Pembroke, Davidson College, East Carolina Technical College, the University of North Carolina in Chapel Hill, Duke University, High Point College, Biltmore College, Elon College, Belmont Abbey, Presbyterian Junior College in Maxton and Lenoir-Rhyne College. North Carolina A&T College was one of six Black colleges in the country selected to participate in the program, graduating fifty out of sixty cadets between 1939 and 1942. Students had to be between the ages of nineteen and twenty-five and have at least one year of college credit. They had to pass physical and educational examinations. Eventually, classes would be offered at several high schools, including those in Fayetteville, Wilmington and Winston-Salem.[83]

There were detractors. Some politicians called the program "New Deal warmongering." Senator J.W. Bailey thought the country "wholly unprepared to enter war as a belligerent." Naval pilot and Raleigh native Andrew Crinkley wrote after the war that the Civilian Pilot Training Program (CPTP) was training students for an "air war" with "make-believe aviators, whose training, and qualifications as Naval aviators, was a farce." The pace to build an aviation arsenal and to properly train pilots, crews, and mechanics, was soon accelerated.[84]

In an attempt to train servicemen, the Carolina Maneuvers was launched. In the fall of 1941, three hundred thousand U.S. troops invaded the Carolinas. They were divided into two teams—the Red and the Blue—with opposing sides wearing colored armbands. This was the second-largest peacetime training program in United States history, involving infantry, airplanes and engineers, along with logistical support. Over seventy P-40 pilots augmented the fighters and light bombers stationed at the Charlotte Air Base. Paratroopers jumped from airplanes and landed on Pope Field. The maneuvers brought a host of famous commanders to the state, including Generals George S. Patton, Hugh Drum (whom Patton captured on the first day), Lesley McNair and George C. Marshall. It was training that was unfortunately soon put to the test.[85]

5

WATCHING THE SKIES AND PROTECTING THE COAST

AVIATION IN NORTH CAROLINA DURING WORLD WAR II

President Franklin D. Roosevelt, in a joint session of the U.S. Congress on December 8, 1941, declared the day before a "date which will live in infamy." On December 7, 1941, Japanese bombers, fighters and torpedo airplanes launched a surprise attack on the U.S. military bases at Pearl Harbor, Hawaii. Over 2,400 American sailors, marines, soldiers and civilians were killed, with more than 1,100 wounded. Numerous naval vessels were destroyed and damaged. The attackers also struck the airfields at Ford Island, Hickam Field and Wheeler Field, destroying 188 airplanes and damaging 159 others. "I had never seen so many planes coming overhead," recalled Selma native Seaman James Lancaster. "When I saw those rising suns under the wings, I knew what was coming." Japan had declared war on the United States, followed by Germany and Italy on December 11.[86]

Aviation in the United States changed immediately, a change that certainly affected North Carolina. All airplanes, except those piloted by military personnel or under government contract, were grounded, along with their pilots. Pilots had to reapply for new licenses, providing two forms of identification, including birth certificates. This left hundreds of pilots stranded across North Carolina as well as across the country. There were new rules. Pilots were required to carry their licenses at all times, and the license had to contain a photograph, fingerprint and signature. Pilots who planned to fly more than ten miles from an airport had to file a flight plan, and commercial pilots were banned from flying within 150 miles of the coast. The new pilot certificates had to be inspected by an official from the

CAA. Guards and police officers were posted at airports, and a clearance officer had to check all incoming and outgoing aircraft, registering the names of pilots and passengers and submitting this information to officials in Washington, D.C., within twenty-four hours. Pilots had the authority to refuse to fly any person whom they did not believe was an American citizen. All airports along the coast were closed to commercial aviation, and all the air markers that the Works Progress Administration had worked so diligently to install were removed or covered up. Commercial aviation in the United States practically ground to a halt, as the needs of the nation took priority.[87]

Just over a month after the attack on Pearl Harbor, the war erupted off the coast of North Carolina. At 1:30 a.m. on January 18, 1942, the *Allen Jackson*, a 430-foot-long tanker bound for New York with almost seventy-three thousand barrels of crude oil on board, was torpedoed 70 miles off Cape Hatteras. It was the first American ship sunk by a German U-boat off the coast of North Carolina during World War II, sent to the bottom of the Graveyard of the Atlantic. Over the next six months, scores of merchant and military vessels were lost off the Outer Banks. Some of these attacks came so close to land that Outer Banks residents could hear the explosions and see the burning wrecks. Ocracoke Island resident Blanche Howard Jolliff recalled that some of the explosions would "shake the houses and sometimes the explosions cracked the cisterns, damaged the sheet rock and plaster in some of the houses." A member of the Civil Air Patrol recalled that on the day she arrived, she "could see ships burning off the coast almost every night. You couldn't walk on the beaches out around Nags Head for the litter from the ships torn apart, from the cases of fruit and the cases of vegetables…the sailor hats, and all these things." While the danger of German U-boat attacks lingered for the duration of the war years, the largest threat lay in the first six months of 1942. More than seventy vessels were sunk just off the coast of North Carolina in those six months. Over 1,700 seaman and civilians lost their lives. One historian argued that these attacks "constituted a greater strategic setback for the allied war effort than did the defeat at Pearl Harbor."[88]

There were simply not enough military vessels and planes to patrol North Carolina's approximately 320 miles of coastline in early 1942. With German U-boats close by, the threat of invasion was a constant rumor to those who lived along that coast. Into this void stepped the Civil Air Patrol. Created on December 1, 1941, the Civil Air Patrol was a nationwide program designed to supplement regular military forces in case of emergency. The North Carolina Wing Civil Air Patrol (CAP) was just one part of the state's

A Civil Air Patrol airplane is pictured on the runway in High Point. *State Archives of North Carolina.*

civilian defense efforts. In Charlotte, the leaders of the Carolina Aero Club contacted Governor Broughton in June 1941 to propose plans on how to use the state's 1,000 licensed pilots as a "civil air reserve." The pilots and support staff were volunteers, while the state paid for fuel, oil, housing and food when the pilots and their planes were on duty. A committee was appointed in September to explore the idea, and on October 25, 1941, a resolution was passed authorizing the creation of a state wing. By January 1942, the North Carolina Wing had 350 members and over 100 aircraft. There was an 80-hour ground school and a 150-hour flying course each pilot had to undergo. Private aircraft were painted bright colors, emblazoned with the CAP-specific roundel. These aircraft, which operated in pairs with a pilot and observer in each plane, would fly low up to sixty miles out over the ocean. They looked for enemy submarines, victims of attacks and mines. Even the presence of a CAP plane would cause a submarine to dive. Once any of these objects was spotted, the information was relayed, and the military aircraft or ships were dispatched to the area. Later, the CAP planes were fitted with one-hundred-pound bombs. Orders and intelligence came from the headquarters of the Twenty-Fifth Antisubmarine Wing in New York to Langley Field in Hampton, which would transmit them to the base at Manteo.[89]

By May 1942, the North Carolina Wing CAP had grown to 400 aircraft and 762 members. While there was a proposal to open a coastal base in Wilmington, work began on CAP Coastal Patrol Base no. 16 on July 22, 1942, at the Skyco Airport at Manteo. The grass airstrip was mowed, brush was cleared and a radio antenna was erected. One new arrival described it as nothing more than "a cow pasture, with a farm house as headquarters." The mosquitos were so bad that the mechanics who serviced the planes had to wear netting. "The men told jokes about how big the mosquitoes were and what they would say to each other like, 'Shall we eat him here or drag him off to the swamp,'" recalled Sergeant Dorothy Graham.[90]

On August 10, 1942, an airplane took off from Skyco for the first patrol. By the end of the month, there were patrols along the North Carolina coast to Ocracoke Inlet from dawn to dusk. In September 1942, the base moved from the old Skyco Airfield to the new airport just north of Manteo, an airport that was constructed by the WPA. The following March, the new airbase was designated the U.S. Naval Auxiliary Air Station Manteo. At the time, Naval Fighting Squadron 17 was also stationed at the base.[91]

A second CAP base was established in Beaufort on September 2, 1942, CAP Patrol Base no. 21. The future base was located just north of town. "There was a nice field, if you had rice planting in mind, almost entirely surrounded by water," one reporting officer concluded. The new base was to patrol the area between Cape Hatteras to Cape Fear. A house that was being constructed on the site was turned into an operations building, while barracks and a hangar were constructed, along with a radio tower. The base officially opened on September 7, with its first flight occurring on September 30. Both bases held more than just pilots and observers. There were men and women there who worked in communications, administration, airdrome and supply and intelligence and as guards, mechanics and engineers. There were 140 men and women who served at only the Beaufort bases, although not all at the same time. The crews from both bases came in from all over the state.[92]

The missions often varied each day that the weather allowed them to fly. Base 21 was in the air on October 3, looking for two navy pilots whose plane had blown up. On November 6, they spotted a sinking schooner with a life raft, including four men and one woman nearby. Radio broadcasts were sent to the navy and coast guard, and the original planes stayed near the target until they ran low on fuel and were replaced by another pair of CAP planes. On November 14, they flew patrol over a convoy, and on February 1, 1943, they were sent to help the coast guard after a submarine sighting. Three days later, a coast guard patrolman spotted a group of men on the beach near Bogue Inlet. Since the men did not stop when hailed, the guardsman shot into the group, forcing them to scatter into the dunes. It was believed the men were German saboteurs deposited by a submarine. The CAP personnel regularly flew missions not just out to sea but also along the beach. Rumors of operatives coming ashore along the Outer Banks were persistent, although never verified, at least in North Carolina.[93]

Flying these various missions could be fraught with danger. In March 1943, two CAP planes were requested to meet a freighter off the New River and escort it north. On approaching the ship in a prescribed pattern, they noticed "tracer bullets crossing the path of the planes." The pilots attempted to change their altitude, but the crew persisted in shooting at them, and the CAP planes left the area. The navy "severely reprimanded" the ship's captain. There were several times that the airplanes were forced down, often because of mechanical problems. In November 1942, pilot Guy Cherry Jr. of Kinston and his observer, George C. Grove of Hickory, were forced to crash-land in the ocean due to engine failure. Over three hours later, they were found by other planes, but rough seas prevented a navy Catalina hydroplane from landing until that evening. In the meantime, Cherry died of exposure and drowning. Grove strapped the young aviator to his back. There were several other casualties, including pilot Harry L. Lundquist and observer David S. Williams, who crashed shortly after their takeoff from the Beaufort base.[94]

While no North Carolina–based CAP airplane is credited with sinking an enemy submarine, there were several sunk by navy fliers. *U-701* was one of the German submarines that patrolled the Cape Hatteras area. The submarine's commander was told that due to the large number of American aircraft observing in the vicinity, the craft needed to stay submerged during the day. Around noon every day, the submarine would come to the surface for a few moments to purge the fouled air aboard before submerging again to lie on the bottom until night fell. As *U-701* started to dive, an aircraft was spotted. It was a Lockheed Hudson Bomber. The submarine was at a depth of 105 feet when depth charges, dropped by the bomber, exploded. Kapitanleutnant Horst Degen, who commanded *U-701*, recalled that the explosion "must have ripped the aft hull to pieces." Water flooded into the stricken vessel as it settled on the ocean floor. The hatch on the conning tower was opened, and sixteen men made their way to the surface. The bomber threw the survivors two life rafts, but they floated away before the German sailors could get to them. At noon on July 7, a blimp spotted the

A U.S. Navy balloon hovers over a raft with German sailors, waiting to be picked up by the coast guard. *National Archives.*

men, now reduced to just four, and a life raft, blankets and water were thrown to them. Later, a U.S. Navy seaplane landed nearby to pick up the four. It had collected three others earlier. The seven were taken to Newport News and held as prisoners for the remainder of the war. Overall, there were four German U-boats sunk off the North Carolina coast during World War II.[95]

On July 9, 1943, the army and navy came to a consensus about aerial support in antisubmarine operations. As soon as the navy was ready, the army would withdraw. Since CAP operations were under army control, the two CAP bases along the North Carolina coast were closed. The Beaufort base was consolidated with the Manteo base, and on August 31, 1943, both were closed. In December 1943, they became Tow Target Unit no. 21 and were transferred to Monogram, U.S. Naval Auxiliary Air Station, Driver, Virginia. At a distance of five thousand feet, the pilots towed canvas targets behind their airplanes for antiaircraft gunnery practice during the daytime and aircraft tracking training at night. Tow Target Unit no. 21 was disbanded on April 15, 1944, and some of the men and planes were assigned to other units.[96]

German submarines found the coast of North Carolina to be a prime hunting ground for several reasons. The Outer Banks jutted well out into the Atlantic Ocean, and the dangerous shoals, winds and waves made it a treacherous area. It was far from defensive bases, which allowed the submarines to spend the night hunting merchant vessels and then to drop into deeper waters to avoid enemy patrols. Furthermore, the coastal villages and towns did not practice blackouts, which allowed the merchant ships to be easily spotted as they moved along the coast. Those blackouts were under the jurisdiction of the Office of Civilian Defense.

President Roosevelt created the Office of Civilian Defense on May 20, 1941. The goal was to coordinate federal and state actions in case there was a war. The volunteer Civilian Defense had many different aspects: organizing scrap drives, promoting Victory Gardens and the Victory Corps and training nursing aides, fire watchers, road repair crews and auxiliary firemen and policemen. Other volunteers under Civilian Defense were air raid wardens.

Every county in North Carolina had its own Civilian Defense Council. The job of the local air raid warden was to patrol the streets during a blackout and make sure no light was visible. Visible light could provide a target for aircraft or submarines. Towns and cities adopted blackout ordinances. Within twenty miles of the coast, all citizens were required to turn off all outside lights and use blackout curtains and blackout headlights from 6:15 p.m. to 7:15 a.m. Various steps were taken to improve the effectiveness of the blackouts. The mayor of Beaufort ventured offshore to see that the lights of his town were extinguished. In several places, such as Gastonia, Southern Pines and Wilmington, CAP airplanes were used to observe the response to the blackout drills. Governor Broughton accompanied one airplane from Pope Field in February 1943 during a blackout drill over Raleigh. For one Washington County blackout, the county deployed twenty air raid wardens, eleven auxiliary police and eight messengers to patrol the county. Those who resisted could be arrested by local law enforcement. Edwin Williams of Fairmont refused to take the necessary steps to comply, and after a crowd of fifty people gathered at his house, he was arrested. Farther from the coast, enforcement was more difficult. When a drill was conducted in Blowing Rock, Louise Wheelwright refused to "to put out lights." When confronted, she told the deputy "I don't believe I will. They are entirely too often and stay on too long. We have a young baby here." Chief of Police D.W. Wooten visited her the next day, and she told him that the blackout drills were "all tom foolery

A poster recruits volunteers for the Civil Air Patrol. *Library of Congress.*

and nothing but a play game. It is not necessary up here in the mountains and she was not going to comply with any signals." After a drill in Gaston County, several did not comply, and warrants were sworn out. However, the air raid warden did not want to serve any warrants, as the offenders were his neighbors.[97]

Another aviation aspect under Civilian Defense was the Aircraft Warning Service (AWS). The AWS served as a human radar system, monitoring aircraft flying over the state. A grid system was developed that included observation posts at predetermined coordinates, with some nine hundred planned posts in North Carolina. A chief observer was appointed for every post, with many other observers there to help alleviate the responsibility for covering many of the posts, some of which were manned for twenty-four hours a day. If the observer spotted or heard an airplane, he filled out a simple form, picked up a telephone and told the operator, "Army Flash." The operator connected the observer to the nearest filter center, and the observer reported to the volunteer on the other end of the line the necessary information: the number of airplanes, how many motors, which direction they were flying, whether the aircraft were high or low and any other observations. If the Army Air Forces personnel at the filter center knew of the flight, then all was good. If the origin or destination of the flight was unknown, then fighter aircraft could be sent to intercept the questionable aircraft. Filter centers in North Carolina were located in Wilmington, Raleigh and Charlotte. Those counties in the far western portions of the state reported to the filter center in Columbia, South Carolina.[98]

In some respects, there seemed to be a rush to volunteer to be aircraft spotters. The Knights of Pythias chapter in Salisbury volunteered for the duty. More than half of the group had served during World War I. Lottie Hood, a college-educated librarian in Vale, wrote to the Third Interceptor Command in Florida, wanting to know the qualifications and requirements for becoming a spotter. Manning the posts could be a family affair. The post in Blowing Rock was located in the yard of Newton C. Greene. He was chief observer. His wife, Emma, and daughter, Doris, were assistant observers. Some areas, however, struggled to get enough volunteers. Forsyth County had twelve posts that needed fifteen to twenty spotters each. They struggled to come up with that number in March 1942.[99]

To help encourage women to volunteer, especially in the filter centers, Adelaide Rickenbacker, the wife of famed World War I flying ace Eddie Rickenbacker, traveled the county as a spokesperson for the Aircraft Warning Service. She was in Charlotte on June 4 and in Wilmington on June 19, touring the filter and information centers. On June 7, she made an address regarding the AWS that was carried on several statewide radio stations. Later in 1942, she visited the information and filter center in Raleigh. After inspecting the center and addressing the crowd, she was invited to tea at the governor's mansion. Mrs. Rickenbacker returned to tour the filter and information center in Wilmington on March 15, 1943, accompanied by famed golfer Robert T. "Bobby" Jones. By November 1943, members of the Women's Army Auxiliary Corps (WAACs) had begun replacing volunteers at the information and filter centers.[100]

There were challenges to overcome. Some locations where observer posts should have been located did not have telephones available, were situated on military bases or were in national forests. Some posts were simply moved a half mile to a better location. A drill in the Wilmington area in December 1941, just after the attack on Pearl Harbor, found that "almost half of the observers contacted by telephone operators had a very disinterested and uncooperative attitude." During the drill, the operators told the observers to activate their posts and place an "army flash" call. Not having access to a telephone was a major obstacle.[101]

Aircraft Warning Service observation posts were located in a variety of structures, from a glass hut on the roof of the Cape Fear Hotel in Wilmington to the water tower on the campus of Lees-McRae College in Banner Elk. Some of the posts were existing fire towers, while in other places, like Enfield, new towers were constructed. Training sessions were held for the spotters, including one in the high school in Lumberton, where slides were shown to observers to teach them how to report airplane sightings. In Raleigh, to help with the recruitment of observers, an exhibit of equipment used by local AWS was set up in the window of the Carolina Power and Light Company. While no German or Japanese aircraft were ever spotted over North Carolina, the AWS did make a difference. The post in Wallace, on the boundary between Duplin and Pender Counties, spotted a plane in distress in February 1943. Despite gas rationing, locals drove their cars to the airport to light the runway with their headlights so the pilot could see to land. A couple of months later in Oxford, an observer noticed an airplane that eventually landed near an orphanage. The chief observer organized a search party that found the plane and pilot, who confessed that he was lost. With the thanks of the government, the Aircraft Warning Service was disbanded in June 1944.[102]

It seemed that almost overnight, North Carolina became an armed military camp. The World War I–era Fort Bragg was rapidly expanded, and bases such as Camp Lejeune, authorized in February 1941, quickly swelled with new construction. Many new military bases were established, some with aviation components, while the majority of civilian airports were partially or completely utilized by military aviators.

Pope Field, Cumberland County

Created in April 1919, Pope Field, adjacent to Fort Bragg, was one of the oldest Army Air Forces landing fields in the United States. The base had undergone upgrades in 1933 and 1934 with the addition of new administrative buildings and residences. Pope Field was one of the training areas for the airborne operations, including glider pilots and C-47 troop transports. These troops were a part of operations in Burma in March 1944 and France in June 1944. Major Charles O. Gordon Sr. recalled that the training at Pope Field was intensive and that they "were subject to call 24 hours a day." Gordon was a member of the 435th Troop Carrier Group. "We made practice drops with [the paratroopers of the 101st Airborne Division] and helped them train for combat. And we flew our gliders a lot, training in many different combat formations." Once overseas, their first combat mission was to drop paratroopers over Normandy on D-Day. William Mitchell was then a pilot in the 53rd Troop Carrier Squadron. While training in North Carolina, Mitchell believed that they hauled paratroopers about 50 percent of the time. After flying about twenty miles from base, they were dropped in a big field. The paratroopers then loaded their parachutes on a truck and hiked back to town. Mitchell found Pope Field rough. "We stocked our own stoves, rummaged through the pinewoods for firewood, and ate GI food in a

A glider being pulled by an airplane on a training mission at Camp McCall. *Author's collection.*

little shed," he told his parents back home. The first mass paratrooper drop took place at Pope Field in 1941, an event witnessed by Generals Marshall, McNair and Clark. In February 1941, a squadron of A-20s from Pope Field located and sank a German submarine off Cape Hatteras.[103]

Seymour-Johnson, Goldsboro

There was much discussion in August 1940 of building a new airport in Goldsboro. The current airport was overcrowded. Federal approval came later that month. A portion of the funds was to come from the WPA, and the rest was to come from the War Department and through bonds issued by the aldermen in Goldsboro. Work got underway in January 1941, and the airport was completed one week before the attack on Pearl Harbor. In October 1942, the Army Air Forces opened the Army Air Forces Technical School at Seymour Johnson. This school trained aircraft mechanics and also offered basic training and pilot training. Later, the base became an overseas placement training center. Some 270,000 men passed through the program during the war years. Albert Williams was one of the mechanics at the base and arrived in October 1943. Williams started as a crew chief on an AT-6A. "An AT-6A is a double seater plane…a cadet training ship….Every pursuit sqd. [squadron] has one," Williams wrote. "We have in our sqd. [squadron] 30 P-47s, 1 AT-6A (that's mine temporarily) 1 BC 13 A, 1 Taylor Cub and a C-78-U. The BC, AT and Cub are used for the purpose of acquainting the pilots with the controls of different ships so that if they are in combat and no P-47s were available, they would be able to fly any pursuit ship if they had to." Williams later moved up to become an assistant crew chief on a P-47. "I like the kind of work I am doing and learning something every day."[104]

Burton Wilder arrived at Seymour Johnson Field in the spring of 1944. He had already earned his wings and was being trained to fly the P-47 Thunderbolt prior to being sent overseas as a replacement combat pilot. Ground school came first, followed by a blindfolded visit to the cockpit of the fighter to demonstrate that he could find all of the controls. On the day of his solo flight, the crew chief helped strap him in and adjusted his headset. Wilder then cranked up the P-47 and taxied down the runway. After completing his preflight checks, Wilder "held the brakes and revved the engine up to maximum power. With the canopy open, the noise was deafening." The canopy was left open during takeoff and landing in case the pilot needed to escape in the event of a crash. He released the brake and sped off down the runway. Once he reached an airspeed of eighty miles per hour, Wilder pulled back on the control stick and went airborne. A short time later, he returned to the paved runway. His flight training at Goldsboro included "tight four-plane combat formation flying and low-altitude flights…sometimes even below tree-level." Later, Wilder was transferred to Bluthenthal Field for training in "dive-bombing, ground strafing and aerial gunnery."[105]

Camp Mackall, Richmond County

A new airfield in Richmond County was approved in March 1941, with the WPA providing $100,000 and the county granting $10,000. The cities of Rockingham and Hamlet each contributed $3,000. After the attack at Pearl Harbor, the U.S. Army took over the property, and the airfield was greatly expanded. Camp Hoffman, later Camp Mackall, opened in 1942. The camp was located near Hoffman, not far from Fort Bragg and the Laurinburg-

The landing strip, hangar and tower at Camp Mackall can be seen in this World War II–era image. *State Archives of North Carolina.*

Maxton Airport. At its peak, Camp Mackall held over 30,000 troops. Eventually, there were 3 five-thousand-foot-long runways, plus numerous supporting buildings, 1,700 in number. Two hangars were constructed to conduct repairs on the gliders used in training the paratroopers. After gliders were proven to be useful, there were often scores or hundreds of airplanes and gliders in the air. One common operation was for C-47s to take off at night, fly to Asheville and return, before releasing gliders over Camp Mackall. Many paratrooper battalions that later earned fame passed through Camp Mackall, including the 506th, whose Easy Company was featured in the Stephen Ambrose book and HBO series *Band of Brothers*, and the 555th, the first all-Black paratrooper battalion, known as the Triple Nickels. Some of these groups, including the 555th, returned to Camp Mackall after their European tours were finished.[106]

Charlotte Air Base

Thanks to the efforts of Mayor Ben Douglas, Charlotte became home to one of the new Army Air Corps airfields in June 1940. Morris Field was selected, with the army signing a twenty-five-year lease that allowed the city to operate the municipal terminal. The army constructed new buildings to house aviators, crews and support staff while widening and lengthening the runways. A control tower was constructed to manage all of the flights. One of the primary missions for the Charlotte Air Base was the continued training of new pilots. Many of the groups that were first stationed at Charlotte Air Base moved on to various theaters of the war. The Fifty-Sixth Pursuit Group, later designated the Fifty-Sixth Fighter Group, was stationed at Charlotte for several months in 1941. By the spring of 1943, they were flying missions over France. The Fifty-Sixth Fighter Group, members of the Eighth Air Force, destroyed more enemy aircraft in combat than any other fighter group in the Eighth. Other groups rotated in and out of the base. While members of the Forty-Sixth Bomb Group spent most of their service flying antisubmarine and search missions over the Gulf of Mexico, many of the pilots had been transferred in from overseas combat groups. The Forty-Sixth arrived in Charlotte in the late fall of 1943. Their mission was to train new pilots to fly the Douglas A-20 Havoc and, later, B-25 Mitchell bombers. Joseph Rutter was one of those replacement pilots, and he arrived in February 1944. After ground school, he moved to the flight line, flying "both day and night…at both medium and low altitude. The combat veterans serving as

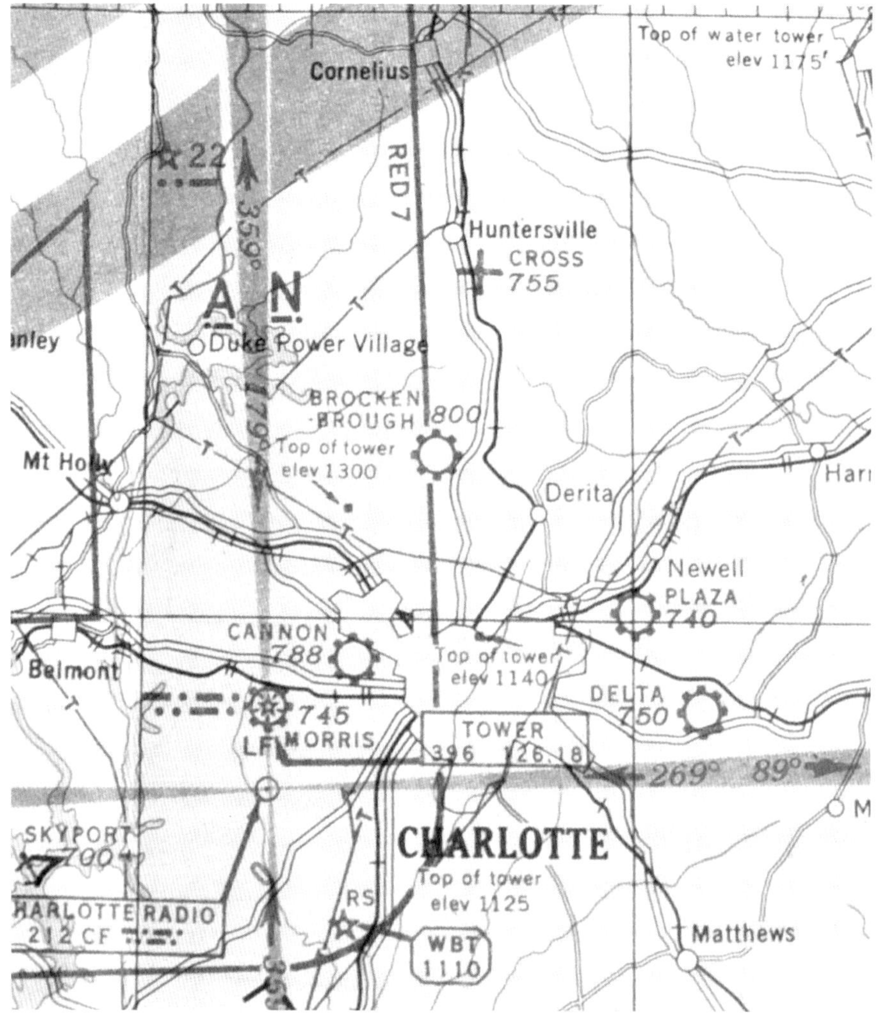

As designated on this 1945 Sectional Aeronautical Chart, Mecklenburg County had five airports and a landing field. *Author's collection.*

our instructors had some different ideas about formation flying than we had previously been exposed to….When they said low level, they did not mean five hundred feet." Rutter had to put in fifteen hours of both night flying and instrument flying. They often followed lighted beacons and Morse code signals between Atlanta and Richmond. When Rutter finished his training, he had amassed over 166 hours of flight time. The Charlotte Air Base was deactivated in May 1945 and officially deeded back to Charlotte a year later. Over $6 million was spent on the property during the war.[107]

WILMINGTON/BLUETHENTHAL ARMY AIRPORT

The day after the attack on Pearl Harbor, P-40 fighters arrived at Bluethenthal Field. Two months later, there were bombers stationed at the field. Eventually, the airbase grew to 1,200 acres, and pilots stationed there not only patrolled the coast but also trained P-47 Thunderbolt fighter pilots. Three seven-thousand-foot-long runways were constructed, and pilots protected the coast and towed targets for antiaircraft training. At the end of the war, the air base was turned back over to the Wilmington–New Hanover County Airport Authority.[108]

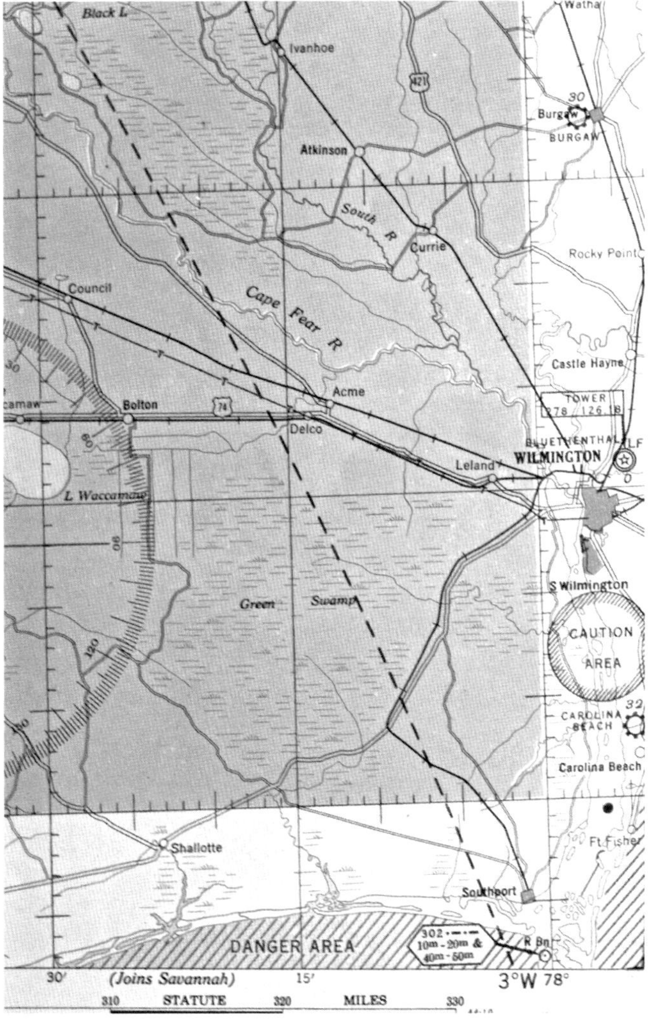

Landing fields in Wallace, Burgaw, Wilmington and Carolina Beach appear on this 1945 sectional aeronautical chart. *Author's collection.*

CAMP DAVIS, ONSLOW COUNTY

The construction at Camp Davis, located in Holly Ridge, Onslow County, began in December 1940. The base was built to train men in the use of barrage balloons, antiaircraft batteries, searchlights and radar equipment. Barrage balloons were large, uncrewed balloons that were used to defend ground targets against air attack. The idea was that the warplanes would become entangled in the steel cables that tethered the balloons to the ground. The barrage balloon school opened in April 1941 and trained both enlisted men and officers. Nine months after opening, the U.S. Army's Barrage Balloon Training Center was ordered to relocate to Camp Tyson, Tennessee. Radar was a revolutionary, top-secret technology that was less than a decade old in the United States at the time. Radar waves were transmitted out, and when they came in contact with an object, they were bounced back to the receiver. Both aircraft and ships could be detected using radar. Searchlights were then used after the radar detected an object in the sky. Powerful beams could

WASP head to the flightline at Camp Davis, ready for a day of towing targets. *Texas Women's University.*

Famed aviatrix Jackie Cochran addresses the WASP at Camp Davis. *Texas Women's University.*

spot ships and allowed antiaircraft guns to zero in on targets. Antiaircraft guns, like 50-caliber machine guns and 40-millimeter, 90-millimeter and 120-millimeter cannons, produced shrapnel fields in the sky, designed to bring down enemy airplanes.[109]

To train these various branches of antiaircraft defensive soldiers, targets were needed. Camp Davis grew to 45,538 acres and included two 5,000-foot runways. Plus, an additional airstrip was constructed at Fort Fisher, south of Wilmington, known as the Fort Fisher Army Air Field. The Third and Fourteenth Tow Target Squadrons were stationed at the airfield, flying A-24s, A-25s and B-34 bombers, many of which had already seen hard service overseas. Their targets were windsocks connected to a cable that was released after the plane took off and trailed behind some 2,400 feet. Crews flew 1,400 feet above the ocean, up to 3 miles out to sea, while the gunners practiced firing at their targets. Pilots and crews at Camp Davis were flying more than 1,200 hours a month by March 1943. With a shortage of male combat pilots, a new group of aviators took over much of the flying at Camp Davis: the Women's Air Service Pilots (WASP).[110]

Above: A WASP checks the engine of Curtiss A-25A at Camp Davis. *National Archives.*

Opposite: Members of the WASP make last-minute checks of their charts before taking off from Camp Davis. *National Archives.*

Originally recruited to ferry planes from manufacturers and repair facilities, twenty-five WASP were called to Washington, D.C., in July 1943. They met with program director Jacqueline Cochran and General Henry "Hap" Arnold in the Pentagon. A day later, they were on their way to Camp Davis, and they were soon training to fly the airplanes that towed the targets for gunnery practice and tracking by radar and searchlights. Eventually, fifty-two WASP were assigned to Camp Davis. They encountered problems with the base commander, who told them they should "go home and knit socks for the troops." The WASP members who served nationwide often faced this same type of discrimination, despite the vital and dangerous jobs they performed for the war effort. One WASP, Ann Baumgartner Carl, recalled, "When towing a target sleeve, it was sobering to realize that the queer round blots of smoke outside the window were live ammunition exploding a bit ahead of target." Several planes returned with shrapnel holes in them, a testament to how closely the rounds exploded. "Then at night we flew searchlight missions," Carl continued. "[W]e flew a racetrack pattern at different altitudes while the artillery man tried to spot and follow us.... This was essentially instrument flying. If you looked outside at the blinding light you lost your night vision and you couldn't even read the instruments."

260881
2110

Pilot Laurine Nielsen tows a target for antiaircraft training off the North Carolina coast. *Texas Women's University.*

Several of the WASP received training to fly the PQ-8 and PQ-14 radio-controlled drones. Two WASP were killed in flying mishaps while at Camp Davis: Mabel Rawlinson on August 23, 1943, and Netty Taylor Wood on September 9, 1943. The antiaircraft battery school at Camp Davis was closed in October 1944, with the pilots assigned to other bases. The WASP program was canceled and disbanded in December 1944.[111]

U.S. MARINE CORPS AIR STATION, CHERRY POINT

Described as "a vast stretch of swamplands," the Marine Corps Air Station at Cherry Point was opened in May 1942. The primary airfield was unofficially named Cunningham Field, in honor of Lieutenant Colonel Alfred A. Cunningham, the first marine aviator. A 1946 history claimed that this was the largest paving project "in the history of mankind," with more than 500,000 cubic yards of concrete and 5,431,500 square yards of asphalt. The latter equated to 242 miles of 20-foot-wide road. Over 4,300 buildings were constructed. Airplanes were both assembled and repaired at the base. New pilots continued their training at Cherry Point, often under the tutelage of combat veterans. The site was considered the "largest marine airfield in the world." There were several marine airfields in the surrounding areas that provided support for Cherry Point. These included Out Lying Field Greenville, Pitt County; Out Lying Field Mitchell, Craven County; Out Lying Field Oak Grove, Jones County; Point of Marsh Target Airfield, Piney Island, Carteret County; Marine Corps Out Lying Field, Atlantic, Carteret County; Marine Corps Auxiliary Landing Field Bogue, Carteret County; Marine Corps Auxiliary Air Field Kinston, Lenoir County; and Marine Corps Air Station New River, Onslow County. Marine Corps Air Station Cherry Point continues to operate today. Some of the auxiliary fields, like Greenville, now the Pitt-Greenville Municipal Airport, were returned to the public sector after the war. Marine Corps Auxiliary Air Field Kinston was closed in October 1945; it was reopened during the Cold War but closed again in 1957. It was finally reopened as the Kinston Regional Jetport. Marine Corps Out Lying Field Mitchell is now the Coastal Carolina Regional Airport. Other sites are still operational, like Atlantic and Oak Grove. Point of Marsh Target Airfield now serves as a target range.[112]

Two marine corps aircrewmen, an aerial gunner and an aerial photographer, stand by their PB4Y-1 patrol bomber at Cherry Point, circa 1943. *National Archives.*

Laurinburg-Maxton Army Air Field

As early as 1920, Maxton had an airfield. In 1933, it was included as one of thirty-three airfields in North Carolina. Maxton's airfield was being used in CAA primary training, in conjunction with the Presbyterian Junior College in 1940. The Laurinburg-Maxton Army Air Field was established in August 1942. The 4,644-acre base featured three 5,000-foot-long runways, with over 500 acres serving as a landing field for gliders. At its height, the base was the largest glider base in the world. The testing of various aircraft was conducted at Laurinburg-Maxton. Chaplain Robert W. Tindall recalled that "not only P38s, but A20s, B25s, B26s, and perhaps other multiengine aircraft were tested as potential towships. Of course C47s and C54s towed the gliders that were eventually used in airborne assault operations." Two of the deadliest crashes that occurred in North Carolina during World War II took place at or near this base. On June 7, 1943, a C-47 took off from Pope Field and crashed within sight of the Laurinburg-Maxton Field, killing all twenty on board. In September 1943, another plane, which was carrying passengers between Pope Field, Lauinburg-Maxton Field and Stout Field in Indiana, crashed on takeoff, killing all twenty-five on board. The field was turned over to local officials at the end of the war.[113]

Raleigh-Durham Army Air Field

Work began on a new airport in Raleigh in 1940, when 891 acres were purchased by the state. Construction on the field was barely underway when Pearl Harbor was attacked. Taken over by the army, the airport was redesignated as the Raleigh-Durham Army Air Field. The field became operational on May 1, 1943. It had three runways and barracks. Eastern Airlines continued its commercial operations during the war years, with up to ten daily flights by mid-1944. Pilots were trained at Raleigh-Durham in Taylorcraft L-2, L-3 and L4 light aircraft, which were to be used to transport wounded soldiers out of the Burma theater. These aircraft were also used as liaison aircraft. One postwar article stated that this field was used by the 158th Liaison Squadron, "a training unit for all liaison squadrons in the Third Air Force." The base was placed in inactive status in December 1944, designated surplus in October 1945 and turned over to civilian officials shortly thereafter.[114]

Asheville-Hendersonville Army Air Field

The Asheville-Hendersonville Airport underwent numerous improvements just prior to the war. In conjunction with Biltmore College, the CAA offered pilot training. The Asheville-Hendersonville Airport continued limited civilian operations, even as the Army Air Corps stepped in to lease the facility for the duration of the war and six additional months. The landing strips were improved, and lights were installed. By the spring of 1942, Asheville had become home to the Army Air Forces Weather Wing. There were eight weather squadrons located across the United States, with the headquarters ensconced in the courthouse in Asheville. These groups gathered information from aircraft, ships, ground weather stations and volunteers. The information was then transmitted to various bases. The job of ferrying officers from the Weather Wing, when needed, eventually fell to Women's Air Service Pilots (WASP). Ten WASP reported to the Asheville-Hendersonville base in November 1943 for thirty days of training, including a refresher course in meteorology. They were then checked out in the aircraft used by the Weather Wing, mostly AT-17s and UC-78s. Three were assigned to Asheville, with the others heading to different Weather Wing squadrons. Like their fellow WASP at Camp Davis, the Asheville pilots were paid $250 per month but were not considered military pilots.[115]

The greater Asheville area played an important role in the war, from the contributions of local manufacturers to the amenities of the Grove Park Inn, which housed Axis diplomats and their families while they awaited deportation and later served as both an army and navy redistribution station, where military personnel could relax before they were assigned to other duties. Quite possibly the biggest wartime excitement to occur in the area came in August 1943, when Captain Robert Morgan, who was from Asheville, brought the *Memphis Belle* to town. Early in the war, pilots and crews who completed twenty-five missions were sent back home. The *Memphis Belle* was a Boeing-built B-17 bomber, and its crew was considered the first bomber crew to complete their twenty-five sorties, flying bomber runs over targets in France and Germany. On completing their last mission, the crew flew the plane back to the States, where they made a tour of facilities and airports as a morale boost for the population. *The Asheville Citizen-Times* ran a special "*Memphis Belle* Homecoming Section," which gave a map of the Asheville-Hendersonville Airport, marked where the bomber would be parked and described the battle scars of the plane. An itinerary was given and included the parade in Asheville, a ceremony in front of the Battery

Following the completion of their twenty-fifth mission, the crew of the *Memphis Belle* returned the B-17 to the States for a tour. *National Archives.*

Park Hotel, a luncheon at the George Vanderbilt Hotel, a radio address and a banquet at the Grove Park Inn. Morgan recalled buzzing the Biltmore Forest County Club Golf Course on the way to the Asheville-Hendersonville Airport. As the bomber and its crew headed out on August 13, Morgan decided to fly over the city "and give them a little good-bye salute." As Morgan approached the tall buildings, he "banked the plane and put the left wing right down between the Courthouse and City Hall. It was kind of a tight fit, but we made it," he recalled. Asheville was the only city in North Carolina the *Memphis Belle* visited.[116]

SMITH REYNOLDS AIRPORT, WINSTON-SALEM

Like other North Carolina airfields, Smith-Reynolds Airport in Winston-Salem was used to train pilots, some one thousand of them. The airport offered the CAA-approved Civil Pilot Training program in mid-1941, with classes provided by Piedmont Aviation. Students were assigned to the program from across the nation and stayed at various places in the city, like the YMCA. The program was one of the few in the nation not tied to a local college. As the war evolved, the classes were expanded. In 1942, the airport was expanded and its runways lengthened.[117]

Greensboro–High Point Municipal Airport

Lindley Field in Greensboro had a storied history: Charles Lindbergh visited in 1927, and the first air mail stop was conducted there the following year. Known as the Tri-Cities Airport, the field was closed during the Depression, and with WPA funds, it was reopened in 1937 as the Greensboro–High Point Municipal Airport. From March 1943 to May 1944, Greensboro served as an Army Air Forces Basic Training facility. Some 87,500 men passed through the four- or eight-week training bootcamp. In May 1944, the training camp ceased operations and became the primary Overseas Replacement Depot on the East Coast. Lindley Field was used by the marines, navy and Army Air Corps as a refueling stop, and it later trained bombers and fighters. The facility was returned to civilian control in August 1945. The airport was greatly improved, with longer runways, lighting for night landings and a control tower.[118]

Work progressed on new hangars at the Greensboro–High Point Airport during World War II. *Albert Barden Collection, State Archives of North Carolina.*

The new hangar at the Greensboro–High Point Airport. *Albert Barden Collection, State Archives of North Carolina.*

COAST GUARD STATION, ELIZABETH CITY

There were many U.S. Coast Guard stations up and down the Outer Banks. They had started as Life Saving Stations, designed to watch for ships wrecked on the dangerous shoals and rescue their crews and passengers. In 1915, the U.S. Coast Guard was created to take over the Life Saving Stations' responsibilities. During the war years, the coast guardsmen patrolled the beach, looking for survivors and saboteurs. The U.S. Coast Guard Air Station at Elizabeth City was commissioned in August 1940. For the war, the base fell under U.S. Navy control. Those who staffed the station were to patrol the coast, looking for enemy submarines and survivors of U-boat attacks. Most of the station's aircraft were seaplanes. Usually, when survivors were spotted, the seaplanes radioed ships to come rescue the survivors. Occasionally, the seaplanes did land on the open ocean. On May 1, 1943, a coast guard plane landed near thirteen survivors who had been at sea for six days. They loaded two critically ill sailors and flew them to Norfolk while a coast guard cutter picked up the others. In July 1942, a coast guard seaplane rescued seven German sailors whose submarine had been sunk. This base reverted to coast guard control after the war. There were several other Naval Auxiliary Air

Stations, such as Harvey Point in Perquimans County, which was used as a navy seaplane training base, and Manteo, which was used to train fighter pilots and served as a base for the Civil Air Patrol.[119]

Weeksville Naval Air Station (LTA)

Construction began on the Weeksville Naval Air Station in August 1941, and the base was commissioned in April 1942. This base housed blimps or lighter-than-air (LTA) craft for antisubmarine patrols. With a crew of eighteen, LTA craft could stay aloft for thirty-eight hours and had a range of 220 miles. Blimps were armed with both machine guns and depth charges. Two hangars were constructed, mammoth structures that housed numerous airships, each 252 feet in length. The base housed airplanes for a while after the war and then closed in 1957. A welder's torch set fire to one of the hangars in 1995, destroying the structure. The other dirigible hangar survives, but the property is now privately owned.[120]

Knollwood Field, Pinehurst

Leased by the U.S. Army Air Corps, Knollwood Field was used as a communication training base and for airborne training. In December 1943, a training exercise known as the Knollwood maneuver was held in the area. Defending the airport and surrounding areas were portions

Several military aircraft, including a Stinson L-5 of the Seventy-Second Liaison Squadron, were parked at Knollwood Air Base on September 14, 1945. *The Lloyd R. Lyckman Photographs and Papers/The Museum of Flight.*

of the Seventeenth Airborne Division, while the attacking force was the Eleventh Airborne Division. Numerous airfields in the area, including Pope Field and the Laurinburg-Maxton Army Air Base, were staging areas for the airborne assault. On December 6, 200 C-47s, loaded with eighteen paratroopers and towing 234 Waco Cg-4A gliders, began the assault. The assault was a resounding success and cemented the role of airborne forces in future military operations. James Bryce, a liaison pilot, recalled training at Knollwood Field. They were based there and practiced landing in outlying fields, as they needed to learn to land in "odd places."[121]

SIMMONS KNOTT AUXILIARY AIRFIELD, NEW BERN

With a 3,200-foot-long runway, this airfield was used by U.S. Marine Corps aviators to practice landing the F4U-1 Corsairs.[122]

BARCO FLIGHT STRIP, CURRITUCK COUNTY

Barco Flight Strip was constructed by the U.S. Army Air Forces as an emergency landing field for aircraft on training flights. The field was closed after the war and used as a drag strip. It is now known as the Currituck County Airport or Currituck Regional Airport.[123]

MARINE CORPS AIR STATION, EDENTON

In May 1942, the U.S. Navy began the construction of an airfield southeast of Edenton. With three paved six-thousand-foot-long runways, the field was used by the marine corps until 1945. Various fighter squadrons used the base for training, while classes in celestial navigation were offered. The first Marine Corps Women's Reserves reported to the base in August 1943. The U.S. Navy took over the base in March 1945. The air group assigned to the USS *Lake Champlain* trained at the base until June 1945. The base was placed in caretaker status in July 1946 but was still occasionally used by the marine corps. It was reestablished by the navy in August 1955, disestablished in December 1959 and once again used by the marine corps until the base was closed, declared surplus and acquired by the Town of Edenton. It then became known as the Northeastern Regional Airport.[124]

A U.S. Marine Corps Women's Reserve celestial navigation training class celebrated graduation day at U.S. Marine Air Station Edenton. *State Archives of North Carolina.*

Pre-Flight Naval School, Chapel Hill

In February 1942, it was announced that the University of North Carolina–Chapel Hill had been selected to host one of the four U.S. Navy preflight training facilities. The university housed and fed the new recruits while receiving funding from the federal government. Several buildings on campus were renovated to accommodate the cadets. One out of four cadets failed to graduate. Classes were offered to prepare students both physically and mentally. These included cockpit instruction and naval aircraft tactics. Gerald Ford was one of the instructors and coaches at the school, as was Paul "Bear" Bryant; some of the famous cadets included George H.W. Bush, Ted Williams and Charlie "Choo Choo" Justice. Gerald Ford actually took private flying lessons while he was stationed at Chapel Hill. The program came to an end in October 1945. Over eighteen thousand cadets passed through the program.[125]

Students at the navy preflight school, University of North Carolina at Chapel Hill (*left to right*): Blaine Hall, George H.W. Bush, Bill Robinson and Dean Phinney. *George Bush Presidential Library and Museum.*

North Carolina contributed in many other ways during the war years. There were numerous war industries across the state, from the ship builders in Wilmington to the textile mills in Glencoe and Burlington. Burlington Mills alone produced more than fifty products for the war effort. There were a couple of industries tied directly to aviation: the aluminum plant in Badin and mica mines in the Toe River Valley. Aluminum is three times lighter than steel but just as strong. The Carolina Aluminum Plant in Badin smelted and rolled enough of the resource to produce 6,000 B-29 bombers. There was even talk of placing an airstrip near Badin in 1940, but that did not appear to happen until after World War II ended. Mica is a nonmetallic mineral used as a thermal and electric insulator in radios and generators in airplanes and automobiles. Prior to the war, mica was imported from India. When the war in the Pacific erupted, that source was no longer available, and domestic production stepped in. Each medium-sized bomber contained five pounds of processed mica. Seventy-five percent of that mica was mined in western North Carolina, namely in Avery, Mitchell and Yancey Counties. In Mebane, Fairchild Aviation established a facility in Burlington to build 475 AT-21 training aircraft. The first AT-21 took flight in May 1943. However, the company failed to meet deadlines. An investigation revealed the company

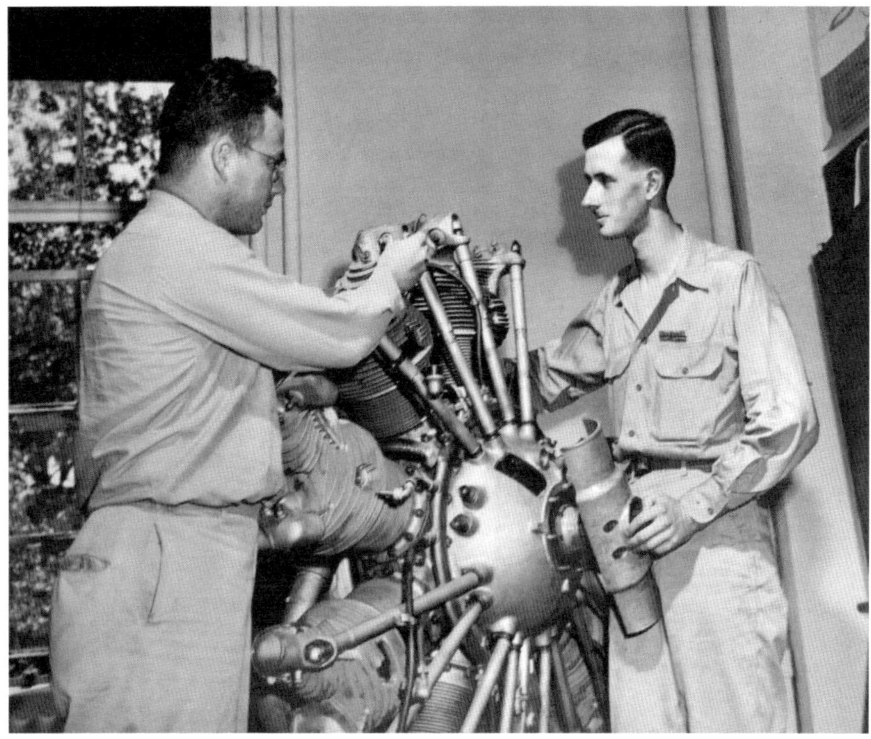

Lieutenant Philippe H.X. de Gaulle (*right*), the son of French General Charles de Gaulle, received naval preflight training at Chapell Hill. *United States Navy.*

suffered from "general waste, inefficiency and extravagance." More than $13 million was spent on that one airplane. The company curtailed operations in mid-1944, closing shortly thereafter.[126]

Another interesting aspect of the war was resolved in the courts. Thomas L. Causby had lived for years on a piece of property that was near the runway at the Greensboro–High Point Airport. An increase in military air traffic wreaked havoc on Causby's chicken farm. Bombers, trainers and fighters flew at all times of the day and night just sixty-three feet from the top of his barn. The glare of the lights and noise from the engines so frightened the chickens that they flew into the walls of the coop and killed themselves. Those that were still alive laid so few eggs that the Causbys gave up their poultry farm. Plus, the air traffic took a toll on the family as well, depriving them of their sleep. In 1944, the Causbys petitioned the courts, asking the government to buy their property. This evolved into a lawsuit—for trespass by air. Causby was awarded $2,000 in damages. However, the Supreme Court ruling became a landmark case in the United States. Prior to the decision, common law held that landowners owned all of the land beneath their property and all of the sky above their property "into the periphery of the universe." The Supreme Court ruled that instead of reaching into the "periphery of the universe," the "landowner owns at least as much of the space above the ground as he can occupy or use in connection with the land." All space above what the landowner can use is in the public domain. Otherwise, airlines and the government would constantly be in danger of trespassing.[127]

NORTH CAROLINIANS SERVING IN WORLD WAR II AVIATION OUTSIDE THE STATE

There were numerous North Carolina natives, both men and women, who became pilots during the war. North Carolina contributed twelve WASP, twenty-five Tuskegee Airmen and three members of Doolittle's Raiders, plus others who flew bombing runs over Europe and carried supplies over the Hump in the Burma Campaign. Many of those pilots started in the Civilian Aeronautics Association's Civilian Pilot Training Program, which began in 1938. The program evolved with the times. In the summer of 1941, women were no longer accepted in the CPTP. All men who entered the program had to pledge to join the military when called. The age requirement was dropped to eighteen, and married men could apply. Uniforms with CAA on the collar were issued. Those who did not meet the standards to become combat pilots could join the program to become cargo or glider specialists, instructors or copilots. At the end of 1941, the program's name was changed to the CAA War Training Service. The program was dissolved by the end of 1944. Many North Carolina wartime pilots started flying through this program. Graham Smith of Hertford County was one of those pilots. He went through training while he was a student at North Carolina A&T. After additional training at Tuskegee Army Air Field, he earned his wings in July 1942. Smith was assigned to the 99th Fighter Squadron, one of the three all-Black fighter squadrons that served during World War II. His brother Reginald served in the 332nd Fighter Group.[128]

Air evacuation units represented another branch of aviation-connected service in which North Carolinians served. Onslow County native Virginia Reavis was one of the nurses in these units. She was training to be a nurse in Lumberton when the war started. After graduation, she worked in the Sixty-Fifth General Hospital before she was selected for air evacuation. After six months of training, she was shipped to England. Cargo planes

Victor Borge and his orchestra visited both Raleigh and Cherry Point in October 1945. *Author's collection.*

were converted to air ambulances. They ferried supplies over and brought the wounded back. Before D-day, Reavis made transatlantic runs, bringing patients back to the States to free up room in English hospitals. Reavis was often the only nurse on flights with twenty-four wounded men. Occasionally, the wounded were German prisoners of war.[129]

World War II saw the transformation of American military aviation, from the prewar Army Air Corps to the Army Air Forces and then to the development of the U.S. Air Force as its own branch of the service in 1947. Over 362,000 North Carolinians served in the military during World War II. Many of those served in roles related to aviation as others flew combat aircraft across Europe, North Africa and the Pacific. Others flew transport airplanes, ferrying supplies and the wounded. There were Women's Air Service Pilots, Tuskegee Airmen, flight nurses and thousands of radio operators, bombardiers, mechanics and ground crew members. North Carolina bases like Fort Bragg trained over 2 million service members. It truly was the greatest generation.

6

"YOU CAN GET THERE FROM HERE"

POST–WORLD WAR II COMMERCIAL AVIATION AND THE COLD WAR

The presidential election of 1948 has often been described as one of the greatest election upsets in American history. Vice President Harry S. Truman had replaced Roosevelt when the latter passed away in Georgia in April 1945. Some people thought World War II was lost, and many were asking, "Truman who?" Truman chose to run for re-election against Republican Governor Thomas E. Dewey. Everyone expected the popular Dewey to win, but Truman captured the presidency. A couple of months prior to Truman's election, New Bern pastor Thomas Fryer was in Washington, D.C. Fryer was trying to visit Bern, Switzerland, and was having trouble with his passport. He was encouraged to meet with the president, and his ten-minute appointment turned into an hour-long conversation. During their meeting, Fryer invited Truman to visit his church in New Bern. Five days after the election, Truman flew into the Cherry Point base and then motored to New Bern, where he attended the morning service at the First Baptist Church of New Bern. He then returned to his plane and continued on to Key West. Truman became the first president to visit North Carolina via airplane, and he made several trips. These included the groundbreaking ceremony at Wake Forest College in Winston-Salem and the dedication of the Raleigh monument to North Carolina's three presidents.[130]

For aviation in North Carolina, World War II had created a boom. As the nation transitioned to peacetime, the army began turning over most of the airports in the state to various municipalities. The cities received

Governor W. Kerr Scott (*left*) appeared with President Harry S. Truman (*center*) and Gordon Gray, president of the University of North Carolina (*right*), on October 15, 1951, at the Smith Reynolds Airport. *State Archives of North Carolina.*

modern, up-to-date, paved airfields, many with control towers and various supporting buildings. In 1944, Congress enacted the Surplus Property Act. States received first dibs on surplus materials. An amendment to the act in 1946 still gave government entities top priority in surplus, but now civilians could purchase the property. In October 1946, the Charlotte Regional Office of the War Assets Administration offered more than 500 surplus airplanes for sale at nearby Woodward Airfield in Camden, South Carolina. The planes that were being sold included PT-13 Stearmans, PT-17 Stearmans, N2S Kaydets, PT-26 Fairchilds, UC-43 Beechcrafts, Grumman G-44 Widgeons, T-6 Texans and Stinson AT-19s. Almost 1,200 veterans showed up for the sale. C-47s, known as Douglas DC-3s in the civilian market, were highly desirable.[131]

In 1947, there were forty-six aviation companies registered in North Carolina. Alamance Aviation Service at the new Fairchild Airport in Burlington offered instruction, charter flights, passenger rides, aircraft rentals and air freight hauling. Cannon Aviation Company leased the Hickory

Military aircraft were stored in the blimp hangar in Weeksville in the years immediately following World War II. *Naval History and Heritage Command.*

Municipal Airport in 1940. During the war, the company was a part of the Civilian Pilots Training Program, and in 1942, Cannon's partner, Lenoir-Rhyne College, was listed as one of the three North Carolina educational institutions able to train naval aviators. By July 1944, the Hickory Airport

The Sandy Ridge Airport in Hickory first opened in 1937. *Iredell County Public Library.*

was offering flight instruction to civilians. Passenger service resumed, with South East Airlines making stops in May 1946. Most of these carriers were short-lived. South East Airlines tried to become one of the major statewide carriers, advertising twenty stops between Asheville and Morehead City. Formed in Gastonia in September 1944, the company lasted until May 1947. Tarboro's Carolina Flying Service seems to have existed only between 1946 and 1947. Mt. Holly's Arrowood's Flying Service appears only twice, once in 1947 and again in 1949. Bailey's Flying Service, based out of Madison at the Mayo Airport, sold used airplanes and automobile glass. The company seemed to exist only between 1946 and 1949. Carolina Skyways developed its own airport near Wilmington in November 1944. A former student brought a civil suit against the company in 1948, claiming to have suffered "permanent facial disfigurement in a plane crash while a student pilot" in June 1946. Carolina Skyways disappeared shortly thereafter.[132]

One commercial carrier that survived for several decades was Piedmont Airlines. Starting out as Reynold's Aviation, the company changed its name to the Camel City Flying Service. Winston-Salem native Tom Davis, who had a love for aviation and was a neighbor to the Reynolds family, purchased the carrier in 1940. Davis's love for aviation stemmed partially from seeing Charles Lindbergh land at Miller Field in 1927. Camel City Flying Service Inc. was dissolved and reborn as Piedmont Aviation Inc.

Before World War II started, Piedmont Aviation became one of the largest wholesale airplane distributors in the southeastern United States. Piedmont trained numerous pilots through the Civilian Pilot Training Program and became the first Civil Aeronautics Administration–approved aircraft and engine overhaul shop between Washington, D.C., and Atlanta. As the CPTP came to an end, Piedmont petitioned the Civil Aeronautics Board (CAB) for permission to begin operating nine routes for passenger, mail and express service. Piedmont was proposing to operate feeder lines. The big four, United, American, Trans-World and Eastern, had already secured the rights to fly into the major cities. These feeder lines flew from smaller cities into the major hubs. In April 1947, the CAB granted Piedmont a certificate to operate. After winning a court case against two of the major airlines and a regional airline from Charlotte, with three used DC-3s, the new Piedmont Airlines took flight from Wilmington's Bluethenthal Field on February 20, 1948. In addition to designations with the required tail number, Piedmont named each of its airplanes. The *Kanawha River Pacemaker* left Wilmington, bound for Cincinnati, with stops in Southern Pines, Charlotte, Tri-Cities and Lexington. The plane returned Davis and several dignitaries to Wilmington that evening. A week later, a route from Louisville, Kentucky, to New Bern began, with a stop at the home office in Winston-Salem. A reception and dinner, held in Winston-Salem, celebrated the event, and Governor R. Gregg Cherry spoke. During the airline's first ten months of operation, it flew 39,379 passengers for more than 1.6 million miles.[133]

Many of Piedmont's stops were smaller municipalities: Kinston, North Carolina; Florence, South Carolina; Roanoke, Virginia; and Charleston, West Virginia. Eventually, New York City and Chicago were added. Piedmont grew over time. In 1950, the airline carried 123,953 passengers. Piedmont carried its 1 millionth passenger in 1954 and its 2 millionth passenger two years later. In August 1953, it served 26 airports; in May 1968, it served 47. Other airplanes were added, including Fokker F-27s and Martin 404s, and in March 1967, the first jet joined the stable: a Boeing 727 on the Atlanta–Asheville–Winston-Salem–Roanoke–New York City route. Female stewardesses were hired in 1962. Piedmont became well known for its customer service and the frugality of its owner, Tom Davis. The company prospered. A new headquarters building at the Smith Reynolds Airport in Winston-Salem replaced the World War II–era building that company executives and staff had been using. The new building was constructed by the city, with Piedmont leasing the structure. By 1967, the airline was flying more than fifty thousand miles a day and had 2,300 employees.[134]

Passengers board a Piedmont Airlines plane at an airport in the 1950s. *Pryor Emerson Humphrey Photograph Collection, State Archives of North Carolina.*

A group of passengers stands in front of Piedmont N746N, a Boeing 737 known as the *Great Lakes Pacemaker*. *Author's collection.*

Piedmont outgrew the office building and, in 1970, built a new office to handle reservations with a computer. A new hangar was built to facilitate the Boeing 737s, and attached offices relieved some of the overcrowding. The late 1960s brought turmoil for many airlines. The economy turned bleak, partially due to the cost of the Vietnam War. Workers demanded more pay as inflation soared. Piedmont had ordered new airplanes, and debt at the company was high. Pilots went on strike in 1969. The pilots believed that the new Boeings needed two pilots and an engineer. Boeing had stated that a flight engineer was not necessary. The courts forced the pilots back to work after twenty-nine days. Things were worse in 1970. As a cost-cutting measure, some stops were dropped, like those to Southern Pines and Elizabeth City. Things were better in 1972, and the airline posted its best revenue ever.[135]

The Arab oil crisis hit in 1973. Gasoline for both automobiles and jets became scarce. Piedmont cut back on flights and lowered its speed. While passengers were still flying, fuel prices continued to rise over the next few years. In the late 1970s, there was much discussion of deregulating the airline industry. The argument was that prior regulation under the Civil Aeronautics Act of 1938 was originally good in the early days, but forty years later, it was keeping ticket prices high and hampering airlines from achieving operational effectiveness. Congress passed the Airline Deregulation Act in 1978. When President Jimmy Carter signed the act, it became the first time in history that a United States industry was deregulated. Airlines could charge whatever they liked for tickets, and everyone had access to any route. Lower fares, increased competition and new airlines benefitted the public. There were some benefits for Piedmont Airlines. Major carriers started to pull out of smaller markets like Louisville, Memphis, Roanoke and Knoxville. Piedmont already served these locations and was able to pick up the additional traffic. The airline was also able to start offering direct flights from smaller cities like Raleigh-Durham and Greensboro to places like Boston and Orlando. New jets were purchased, crews and staff were hired and advertising campaigns were increased. Piedmont was billed as "the up-and-coming airline." By 1980, Piedmont was ranked first in on-time performance, and it was one of the airlines with the fewest complaints, just behind Delta.[136]

Recession in the early 1980s, an air traffic controllers' strike in 1981, historic record-high interest rates and fare wars hurt every airline. For a while, Piedmont continued to weather the storm. The hub at Charlotte handled 130 departures a day. By the end of 1984, the airline served 92 cities in 24 states and Washington, D.C. Added that year were the first

An early linen postcard features Smith Reynolds Airport in Winston-Salem. *Author's collection.*

flights to Los Angeles and San Francisco. Piedmont also won the Airline of the Year Award, presented by *Air Transport World* magazine. Other major airlines were recovered enough to start encroaching on Piedmont's home turf. United Airlines already served Charlotte, Raleigh and Greensboro; American Airlines placed a hub in Raleigh-Durham. The Deregulation Act allowed major airlines to merge with other airlines. Piedmont amended its charter in an effort to protect the company, and it began requiring potential buyers to pay for Piedmont's stock in cash based on its market price. There were talks of acquisition in 1989. Norfolk Southern Corporation, wishing to diversify its holdings, attempted to acquire Piedmont Airlines. In the end, it was USAir that completed the deal. Valued at $1.59 billion, it was the most expensive airline merger in history. The airline's headquarters were moved from Winston-Salem to northern Virginia. On August 4, 1989, the last Piedmont flight left Charlotte, bound for Myrtle Beach. A picnic was held in Greensboro at the maintenance hangar for five hundred employes. The jets were repainted by USAir, and many of Piedmont's employees, realizing that the merger with USAir was a backward step for them, left the company.[137]

Another North Carolina carrier that sprang up in the last half of the twentieth century was Wheeler Airlines. Born in Durham in 1943, Warren Wheeler earned his private pilot's license while in his teens. He followed this with his commercial pilot's license to become the first Black American to graduate from the American Flyers School in Oklahoma. Back in North Carolina, Wheeler opened his own flying school and charter service based out of the Horace Williams Airport in Chapel Hill. One of his frequent clients was North Carolina Governor Terry Sanford, who recommended that Wheeler take the pilot's exam at Piedmont Airlines. Wheeler passed. At the age of twenty-two, Wheeler joined Piedmont Airlines. In 1969, Wheeler founded Wheeler Flying Service. The name was later changed to Wheeler Airlines. Commercial and cargo service was offered from Raleigh-Durham to Greenville, Charlotte, Kinston, New Bern, Wilson, Asheville, Newport News, Richmond and New York City. In the early 1980s, Wheeler Airlines averaged more than forty thousand passengers a year before larger airlines began taking over the routes of regional carriers in the late 1980s. Wheeler completely closed the company in 1991 after a disagreement with Piedmont Airlines that involved code sharing. The first Black American to own a commercial airline, Wheeler also strove to hire Black pilots, including the first two Black women pilots to work for a major airline.[138]

EFFECTIVE DECEMBER 15, 1983

You Can Get There From Here!

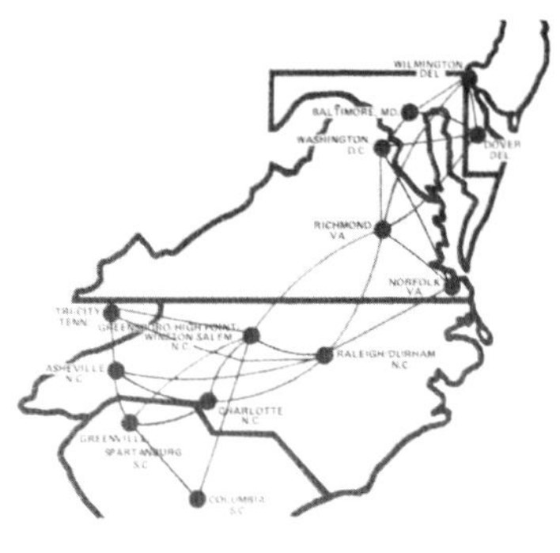

CONNECTIONS TO:
AUGUSTA · CHARLESTON · CHICAGO · CLEVELAND · COLUMBIA · DETROIT · FLORENCE · HICKORY · KNOXVILLE · NEW YORK · PHILADELPHIA · SAVANNAH

CONVENIENT FLIGHTS
linking GEORGIA, the CAROLINAS, VIRGINIA, DELAWARE, MARYLAND, and the DISTRICT OF COLUMBIA

"You can get there from here!" was the slogan on the timetable for Wheeler Airlines. *Author's collection.*

Another innovator was Igor Bensen. Born in Russia, Bensen studied engineering in New Jersey before he landed a job with General Electric. In 1953, he opened the Bensen Aircraft Corporation at the Raleigh-Durham Airport. Bensen bult gyrocopters with a pusher engine. His company sold over ten thousand kits, making his gyrocopters the "most popular home-built aircraft in the world." Bensen set several world records in speed, endurance and altitude with his gyrocopters. He even flew over the Wright Brothers Monument at Kill Devil Hills—twice.[139]

Igor Benson's record-setting gyrocopter is on display at the Stephen F. Udvar-Hazy Center. *Author's collection.*

The Cold War brought new opportunities—and challenges—to aviation across North Carolina. Several World War II facilities were enlarged or repurposed. Other facilities were built as the global situation changed.

The Charlotte Area Missile Plant began its life in 1924 as an assembly plant for the Ford Motor Company. When the Great Depression brought declining sales, Ford closed the factory. It sat vacant until 1941, when it was purchased by the U.S. Army as a new quartermaster depot. The army quickly began constructing several large warehouses and repurposed the old Ford building, turning the facility into one of the largest quartermaster depots on the East Coast. In 1954, the property was leased to Douglas Aircraft, the company responsible for building the Nike antiaircraft missiles. Western Electric in Winston-Salem produced the electronic components, with the final assembly occurring at the Charlotte Area Missile Plant. The plant also produced the Nike B, or Hercules, a missile capable of carrying a nuclear warhead. These missiles were shipped to various compounds across the United States. Douglas Aircraft became the largest employer in Charlotte in 1959. As contracts dwindled and technology advanced, Douglas merged with another company and closed its Charlotte facility in 1967.[140]

With the Soviet Union constructing its own nuclear bombs and with the progress of jet technology, advancements in early warning radar technology also grew. The Air Defense Command was created in 1946, and the next year, there was a proposal for the construction of 411 radar stations and 18 control centers across the United States. That plan was rejected, but the necessity of an air warning defense system grew. At the start of the Korean War, the United States' air defense systems began twenty-four-hour-a-day operations. North Carolina had four radar stations. The Fort Fisher Air Force Radar Station opened in 1955 and was deactivated and closed in 1988; Roanoke Rapids Air Force Radar Station was active between 1956 and 1978; the Winston-Salem Air Force Radar Station was active between 1957 and 1970; and the Cherry Point Air Force Radar Station became operational in 1958 and ceased operations in 1963. Each of these stations had a main building, often "bomb-proof," that housed the radar station, along with numerous support buildings and housing for base personnel. As radar technology evolved, the bases were upgraded. Their original purpose was to provide guidance to interceptor aircraft. The threat of aircraft carrying nuclear payloads waned as intercontinental ballistic missile technology improved, and the bases changed as well.[141]

An official state publication stated that it hoped a war with the Soviet Union could be avoided, but it encouraged civilians to be prepared. The Office of Civilian Defense had ceased operations in 1945, but President Harry Truman reinstated it in 1950, when he signed the U.S. Civil Defense Act. The act placed responsibility for preparedness, in case of nuclear attack, on state and local governments. Each county commission appointed a county director for civil defense. They were charged with organizing and operating a county council made up of a member of the county board, a member of the city council from the largest municipality in the county, a pastor, a county attorney, a leading businessman, a man from a fraternal organization, a "strong women's organization leader" and someone from the press. With the idea that the Cold War could turn into World War III at any moment, numerous fallout shelters, or underground bunkers, were created in just about every county in the state. Some were located in high schools and courthouses, intended to shelter local civilians, while others were constructed in homeowners' backyards. Other shelters were purposely built to house high-value targets, men and material that needed to survive a nuclear blast. One such location was the AT&T facility in Chatham County. Commonly referred to as the "Big Hole," the facility was a multistory underground building that was opened in 1964. The bunker could house government personnel, along with communications equipment that would be operational should a nuclear strike wipe out primary equipment. Another bunker was constructed on Oberlin Road in Raleigh to shelter state employees. There was even a plan to move the justices of the U.S. Supreme Court to Asheville's Grove Park Inn. With the advent of the Emergency Broadcasting System, shelters were constructed underneath radio stations as well. These shelters were stocked with food, water, medical supplies and other items essential to maintain those within for weeks or months.[142]

Another organization directly related to civil defense was the Ground Observer Corps, which was reborn in early 1950, after authorities confessed that low-flying aircraft could avoid detection by air force radar stations. Volunteers across the state were organized into posts that either built observation towers or used existing towers or structures to look for aircraft. The post in Asheville utilized the top of the Buncombe County Courthouse, while observers in Hillsboro were stationed in a nearby fire tower. A "building" was constructed in Mt. Olive for the post, while in Spruce Pine, Boy Scouts constructed a tower atop the town hall. For the system to be effective, posts were needed every eight miles, for a total of 342 posts in the state. Every post needed 168 trained volunteers "to avoid imposition on a few." Like the World War II–era protocol, once a plane was spotted, a call was made and the information was relayed to a filter center. The filter centers for much of North Carolina were located in Charlotte and Durham, and they worked with other centers in Knoxville, Tennessee, and Richmond, Virginia. Over the next few months, various counties held meetings to organize their own Ground Observation Corps posts. There was even a plan to use prisoners in the state's 85 prison camps as spotters. Some posts, like the one at Summerfield, Guilford County, were staffed entirely by women. Charlotte trained Explorer Scouts, while Asheville evidently had a "Negro division" of the Ground Observer Corps. The program, titled "Operation Skywatch," ended in 1958.[143]

Just as they had during World War II, the North Carolina Wing Civil Air Patrol played a role in preparedness across the state. As early as February 1953, CAP partnered with the air force to fly over the several counties in the Charlotte area to test the Ground Observer Corps spotters and related filter centers. This exercise was repeated in Durham and Asheville a few months later. Another role CAP played in supporting civil defense came through the Aerial Radiological Monitoring program. Various radiation detection devices were placed both at airports and in CAP airplanes. The plan was to deploy these airplanes after an attack had taken place to conduct aerial surveys. Once the survey of specific areas was finished, the information would be relayed to emergency operations centers via either personal interview, telephone interview or airdrop if the communication system was overburdened or the radiation levels high. The airplane would then return

As part of the Ground Observer Corps, local Boy Scouts constructed an observer's post at the Spruce Pine Town Hall. *Spruce Pine Public Library.*

to base to be decontaminated. The Aerial Radiological Monitoring program was phased out in 1998.[144]

Another role that CAP continued to perform was the search for lost or missing aircraft. There have been thousands of aviation mishaps over the decades, including planes that have gone down in the mountains and off the coast of North Carolina. In January 1961, a Boeing B-52G Stratofortress based at Seymour Johnson Air Force Base in Goldsboro broke up while in flight not far from the base. Five members of the of the eight-man crew survived. The payload on board the bomber consisted of two MK39 thermonuclear bombs. One of the bombs was quickly found intact. The second bomb had disintegrated after striking the ground at seven hundred miles per hour. Some pieces of the nuclear bomb were recovered, but after teams dug a hole seventy feet down without finding all of the parts of the weapon, the search was called off. CAP units from various parts of the state, including Chapel Hill, flew missions to locate pieces of the plane.[145]

In 1907, the editor of a Wilmington newspaper wrote about a $50,000 prize being offered for a working "aeroplane": "Dear Me, we shall soon be traveling through space." Fifty years later, the Space Race began when the Soviet Union lunched the small satellite *Sputnik I*. North Carolina played a role in that race. In 1956, the Smithsonian Institute began asking for volunteers for Project Moonwatch. Piggybacking on the work of the Ground Observer Corps, Project Moonwatch asked the general public to become amateur scientists and look for man-made satellites as they orbited the Earth. There was "no known radar" that could track satellites. Teams had to register with the Smithsonian, and their information was passed along via shortwave radios. The first teams in North Carolina were the astronomy clubs in Greensboro and Charlotte. The Charlotte team had stations behind the Mint Museum. During a test run in Greensboro, a CAP airplane pulled a light at a certain speed and altitude. In Cary, the team was composed of high school students. When *Sputnik* did pass over North Carolina in October 1957, the stations in the state were ensconced in clouds, although local ham operators did report hearing the beeps emitted by the satellite. Later that week, the director of the Greensboro group reported sighting the satellite. Project Moonwatch continued until the Smithsonian discontinued the program in 1975.[146]

North Carolina's role in the Space Race goes even deeper. Astronauts in the Mercury, Gemini and Apollo programs flew into Chapel Hill and attended stellar navigation classes in the Morehead Planetarium; Burlington

A group of Girl Scouts receive their Wing Scout pins at the Asheville-Hendersonville Airport in March 1950. *Buncombe County Special Collections, Pack Memorial Public Library.*

Mill in Caldwell and Burke Counties manufactured the fabrics used in the heat shields needed for reentry, the Apollo space suits and the flags left behind on the Moon; A-B Emblem in Buncombe County has been making patches for space missions since 1970; the Rosman Satellite Tracking and Data Acquisition Facility in Transylvania County was constructed by NASA as its primary East Coast satellite tracking facility; and the J.A. Jones Construction Company of Charlotte, already famous for constructing military airbases in the Canal Zone in Panama, Liberty ships, World War II airbases and the K-25 and K-27 uranium enrichment process buildings at Oak Ridge in Tennessee, also constructed Launch Complex 17 at Cape Canaveral for the Thor and Delta rockets.

Amid rocket launches, satellite spotting and astronaut training, the first commercial jet in the United States, the Boeing 707, entered commercial service in October 1958. Juan Trippe, the president of Pan American Airways (Pan Am), declared that the jet was the "most important aviation development since Lindbergh's flight. In one fell swoop, we have shrunken the earth."[147]

With larger and faster jet planes, airports had to grow. The World War II–era DC-3s required 2,296 feet of runway to take off. A Boeing 737 needs over 6,000 feet for the same takeoff. Many airports across North Carolina did not have that kind of room or the monetary resources for expansion. Plus, local populations could not support these regional airports, and with the advent of the interstate system and better roads, larger airports close by were within reach. Hickory is just an hour's drive from Charlotte-Douglas International Airport. This eventually led to some airports, like Hickory, Moore County (Pinehurst Regional) Airport and Kinston Regional Jetport, losing passenger service, especially after the Piedmont-USAir merger.

Asheville chose to relocate and moved to a new site about three miles from the old Asheville-Hendersonville Airport. Costing over $2 million, the Asheville Regional Airport, on 740 acres, opened on January 16, 1961. Since then, the runway has been expanded to its current 8,002 feet, and the original 25,000-foot-long terminal was expanded. This airport, managed by the Greater Asheville Regional Airport Authority, is the fourth-busiest airport in North Carolina.[148]

Fayetteville Regional Airport was opened in 1949, with community service provided by Piedmont Airlines. Its improvements in the late 1960s included the lengthening of its runways and a new terminal. A control tower came in 1972, and in 1987, a second concourse was built. Major renovations took place throughout the early 2000s. In 2022, over thirty-three thousand

The old Rosman tracking facility was used by NASA as a primary East Coast satellite tracking facility. *Author's collection.*

A circa-1960 billboard advertises the new Asheville Airport. *Buncombe County Special Collections, Pack Memorial Public Library.*

A Piedmont Airlines DC-3 sits next to the terminal at the Fayetteville Airport. *Author's collection.*

commercial and private aircraft visited the airport, which is served by American Eagle and Delta Air Lines.[149]

Piedmont Triad International Airport (PTI) near Greensboro was able to grow. The site was originally purchased in 1927. It went through several name changes: Tri-Cities Airport, Lindley Field, Greensboro–High Point Airport, Greensboro–High Point–Winston-Salem Regional Airport and, in 1987, Piedmont Triad International Airport. There have been numerous airlines that have serviced the area: Dixie Flying Service, Eastern Air Transport, Piedmont Airlines and Capital Airlines. In 2024, Piedmont Triad International Airport was served by four major passenger companies: Allegiant, American Airlines, Delta and United. Currently, Piedmont Triad has three runways, the longest being 10,001 feet long. Its major improvements started during World War II, with the U.S. Army constructing a second hangar, passenger terminal and control tower. A new passenger terminal was built in 1958, and a third terminal was built in 1982. Piedmont Triad became one of the major aircraft maintenance, repair and overhaul ports on the East Coast. Piedmont Airlines had a facility there, and now, Haeco Americas (formerly TIMCO Aviation Service) and Delta operate there. FedEx, DHL and UPS all operate hubs at the airport, and the global headquarters of Honda Aircraft Company is located there. PTI is the third-busiest airport in North Carolina.[150]

Wilmington International Airport (ILM) began life in 1927 and, in 1928, was named Bluethenthal Field. The U.S. Army built three seven-thousand-foot-long runways there during World War II. In the 1950s, the airport was known as the New Hanover County Airport; then in 1988, it became New Hanover County International Airport; and finally, in December 1997, it became the Wilmington International Airport. A new terminal building, along with a control tower, was constructed in 1950. This building was replaced in 1990. Piedmont Airlines flew passenger service there in 1948. In 2024, the area was served by American Airlines, Avelo, Delta, Sun Country Airlines and United. ILM is the fifth-busiest airport in North Carolina and has a twenty-four-hours-a-day customs ramp.[151]

In May 1943, the new Raleigh-Durham Airport (RDU) opened, with passenger service being provided by Eastern Airlines. The new airport had three runways and a passenger terminal. Following World War II, Capital Airlines, Piedmont Airlines and, finally, Delta Airlines flew from RDU. A new terminal was constructed in 1955, and jet service began in 1965.

The new terminal at Raleigh-Durham Airport was constructed in 1955. *Author's collection.*

Allegheny Airlines joined the fleet of carriers in 1979, followed by Trans World Airlines and American Airlines. A new terminal opened in 1982, and a ten-thousand-foot-long runway came in 1986. New terminal buildings were added, along with international flights. In 2024, the Raleigh-Durham International Airport was served by eighteen carriers and was the second-busiest airport in North Carolina.[152]

Charlotte Douglas International Airport (CLT) opened in 1935 as the Charlotte Municipal Airport. In January 1941, it was renamed Douglas Municipal Airport after Charlotte Mayor Ben Elbert Douglas. It was also known as Morris Field during World War II. The airport was renamed again in 1982 the Charlotte Douglas International Airport. A new two-story terminal was constructed in 1954. In the late 1960s, renovations began that expanded the facility. A new passenger terminal came in 1979, and a 10,000-foot-long runway and control tower followed in 1980. Expansions continued with a new 80,000-square-foot concourse in 1990. In 2009, a fourth runway was completed. As of 2024, CLT had 115 gates on 5 concourses, all located in one 1.8-million-square-foot terminal building. CLT is the largest airport in North Carolina and one of the busiest airports in the United States, with over 110,000 people passing through it every day (a total of more than 53 million in 2023). At 370 feet in height, the new air traffic control tower is the

Families and associates wait at the Charlotte Terminal for guests to arrive. *Author's collection.*

These students are attending an aviation ground school at the Wilson Airport, circa 1950. *State Archives of North Carolina.*

second-tallest tower that falls under the jurisdiction of the Federal Aviation Administrations.[153]

Even municipal airports still play a vital role. During the catastrophic damage left in the wake of Hurricane Helene in September 2024, airports, such as those in Hickory and Salisbury, served as vital staging areas for supplies that were transported by small airplanes and helicopters to sites like the Boone Airport and Avery-Morrison Airport. Critical airlifts of supplies and evacuations of storm victims were facilitated by many small North Carolina airports

Aviation in North Carolina is a major industry. There are 72 public airports, 18,469 licensed pilots and 6,628 registered aircraft. In 2023, the aviation industry supported over 28,000 jobs, and there were 20 FAA-approved aviation schools with 3,320 flight instructors. Overall, aviation has a $72 billion annual impact in North Carolina, affecting 330,000 jobs. Numerous aerospace companies have facilities in North Carolina, including Boeing, GE Aerospace, Lockheed Martin and Pratt & Whitney. Over 400 companies supply the aerospace industry with components. In June 2024, Boom Supersonic opened a factory to produce supersonic jets at Piedmont Triad International Airport.[154]

Aviation in North Carolina has come a long way—from the windswept hills along the Outer Banks to a factory manufacturing supersonic jets.

7

A FEW FAMOUS FLIERS FROM NORTH CAROLINA

There have certainly been many North Carolinians who made important contributions to the field of aviation, but there are a few who merit special attention in the history of the state's connection to the sky.

Thornwell H. Andrews (1876–1932), who was born in Charlotte, learned to fly in 1911 in White Plains, New York. In 1912, he became the first person to fly over Charlotte. The City of Charlotte awarded him a gold medal for his actions. Andrews went on to perform all over the United States but retired to Charlotte, where he worked as a mechanic. He passed away after an illness that lasted several weeks and was buried in Elmwood Cemetery in Charlotte.[155]

Eric L. "Polly" Ellington (1889–1913) was born in Johnston County. He entered the U.S. Naval Academy at the age of sixteen and graduated third in his class in 1909. He did several tours until 1911, when he resigned his commission and entered the U.S. Army as a second lieutenant. While stationed in College Park, Maryland, Ellington qualified as a military aviator in August 1912, and he served with the Signal Corps until his death in a crash in San Diego, California. Ellington Field in Texas is named for him. He was buried at the Clayton City Cemetery in Johnston County.[156]

Arthur Bluethenthal (1891–1918) was born in Wilmington, and while he attended Princeton University, he was an All-American football player. He later coached at Princeton and the University of North Carolina. When World War I broke out, Bluethenthal joined the French Foreign Legion and then the French Flying Corps. He was the only American in the Lafayette Flying Corps. While directing artillery fire from a Brequet bomber, he was attacked by German fighters and killed near Maignelay, France. Numerous awards and tributes were paid to him, and in 1921, he was reburied in Oakwood Cemetery in Wilmington. Bluethenthal Field in Wilmington is named for him, and he was posthumously inducted into the International Jewish Sports Hall of Fame.

Killed in World War I, Arthur Bluethenthal was honored as the namesake of the Wilmington airport. *Cape Fear Museum of History and Science.*

KIFFIN ROCKWELL (1892–1916) was born in Newport, Tennessee. His father's family was from North Carolina. When Rockwell was fourteen, his family moved to Asheville, where he attended Asheville High School. He later enrolled in the Virginia Military Institute and was appointed to the U.S. Naval Academy, but he returned to Lexington, where he enrolled in Washington and Lee College, although he never actually graduated. For a time, Rockwell worked as a journalist. In 1914, at the start of World War I, Kiffin and his brother Paul enlisted in the French Foreign Legion. After he recovered from a wound, Kiffin transferred to the French Air Force, and in April 1916, he helped found the Lafayette Escadrille. Not long after, he became the first American pilot to down an enemy plane. Four months later, Rockwell was killed in a dogfight. He was buried in Luxeuil-les-Bains Commal Cemetery in Franche-Comte, France. There is a North Carolina Highway Historical Marker near his home in Asheville.[157]

BELVIN WOMBLE MAYNARD (1892–1922), known as "The Flying Parson," was born in Morven, Anson County. The United States entered World War I while Maynard was a student at Wake Forest Theological School. He enlisted, transferred to the air service and, in France, became a test pilot, testing new aircraft before they were sent to frontline units. Fame came when he recorded performing 318 loop-the-loops without losing altitude. Maynard, on returning to the States, delayed returning to Wake Forest and instead entered a race to fly between Minelo, New York, and Toronto, Canada. He won that race, along with the Double Transcontinental Aerial Derby a couple of months later, earning national fame and setting a new record for transcontinental flight. Maynard fell afoul of the army, accusing some fellow pilots of being intoxicated while flying. On May 8, 1920, he was discharged and worked at the YMCA in Brooklyn and as an aerial photographer. Maynard also married a couple in the cockpit of a plane and broadcast an Easter sermon while flying. In September 1922, he was performing with Trombly's Flying Circus in Rutland, Vermont, when he was unable to pull his plane out of a dive and crashed. While he was not killed in the crash, he died while en route to the hospital. There was a funeral procession through the streets of New York City. Maynard was only twenty-nine years old and left behind a wife and several children. His remains were interred in the Maynard Family Cemetery in Harrells, Sampson County.[158]

GEORGIA ANN THOMPSON "TINY" BROADWICK BROWN (1893–1978) was born in Vance County. She was married at the age of twelve, became a mother at thirteen and was then abandoned by her husband. She then watched Charles Broadwick parachute from a balloon at a carnival in Raleigh. She joined Broadwick's show, adopted his last name and was soon parachuting from balloons at various state fairs, including those in Morganton and Statesville in the summer of 1908. Standing just over four feet tall, she was billed as "Tiny" and "The Doll Girl." In 1913, she became the first woman to parachute from an airplane; as it soared at two thousand feet, she jumped from the craft and landed in Griffith Park in

Belvin Maynard is greeted by a crowd in Raleigh on May 20, 1920. *Albert Barden Collection, State Archives of North Carolina.*

Tiny Broadwick, suspended beside the plane fuselage piloted by Glenn Martin, made over one thousand parachute drops. *State Archives of North Carolina.*

Los Angeles. A year later, she was demonstrating her pack parachute for army officials when her line became tangled in the tail of the airplane. She cut the line and pulled the parachute open by hand, becoming the first person to free-fall parachute jump. After more than 1,100 jumps, she retired from parachuting in 1922. Broadwick was highly decorated in her lifetime, receiving the John Glenn Award and being recognized as the only female aviator of the Early Birds of Aviation. She died in California and was buried at the Sunset Garden Memorial Cemetery in Vance County. A North Carolina Highway Historical Marker is nearby.[159]

John Edison Crowell (1893–1983) was born in Union County. At the age of twelve, he ordered a Blériot monoplane from Heath Aerial Vehicle Company of Chicago and assembled it when it arrived. He later moved to Maryland, where he attempted to get a job at the College Park Airport. Although he was unsuccessful in that job search, he did land a position at Standard Aero Corporation in New Jersey. Following World War I, he returned to Charlotte. Crowell was Charlotte's first licensed pilot and first airport manager, and he set world records in aerobatics while barnstorming throughout the South. He reportedly logged 2.5 million miles in one hundred different aircraft. Plus, he held several patents for various mechanical apparatuses. He established the Plaza Airport, which had two runways and seven hangars. The airport was in operation from the 1920s until the 1950s. Crowell was buried in the Forest Lawn Cemetery in Union County.[160]

Viola Estelle Gentry (1894–1988), the "Flying Cashier," was born in Rockingham County. Gentry learned to fly in 1924 and is credited with being the first woman to fly an aircraft in North Carolina. On December 20, 1928, Gentry flew for eight hours, six minutes and thirty-seven seconds, setting the first non-refueled endurance record for a woman. The record was broken the following year. Gentry tried to reclaim the record in July 1927, but her airplane crashed, killing her pilot Jack Ashcraft. Gentry continued to fly and was an advocate for women in aviation. She was also a personal friend of Amelia Earhart and an original member of the Ninety-Nines. Later, she worked on building the History of Aviation Collection in the Special Collections Department, McDermott Library, University of Texas. In 2022, Gentry was inducted into the North Carolina Aviation Hall of Fame. Gentry was buried in the Leemont Cemetery in Danville, Virginia.[161]

Caleb Vance Haynes (1895–1966) was born in Dobson, Surry County, the grandson of Chang Bunker, one of North Carolina's famous "Siamese Twins." In 1917, he graduated from Wake Forest College with a degree in law. Haynes joined the U.S. Army in 1917 and attended the School of Military Aeronautics at Georgia Polytechnic Institute. During World War I, he served as a test pilot in Tours, and then as an aviation instructor in Issoudun. During the Paris Peace Conference, Haynes was an aide to President Woodrow Wilson. Haynes spent much of the interwar years as an instructor, leading a pursuit squadron, working with air mail and test flying what became the B-17 bomber. He was awarded the Distinguished Flying Cross in 1939 for flying the experimental XB-15 to Santiago, Chile, while carrying emergency supplies for survivors of the 1939 Chillán earthquake. Haynes spent most of World War II flying the Hump, carrying supplies to beleaguered troops in China. After eighteen months in Asia, he returned to the United States and was assigned to the I Bomber Command, First Air Forces, as commanding general and later moved to III Bomber Command. Both groups flew along the coast looking for submarines. Haynes continued in various command roles after the war before retiring in 1953 at the rank of major general. He retired to California, where he passed away, and was buried at Arlington National Cemetery.[162]

ANDREW CRINKLEY (1896–1981) was a naval aviator who was born in Raleigh and served in both World Wars, attaining the rank of captain. In 1921, he set a world record for seaplane endurance, flying from San Diego to Panama. Crinkley taught at the naval flight school in Pensacola; was stationed on board the USS *Houston*, then in Manila, Philippines; and later served as a test pilot. During World War II, he served as the assistant naval attaché to the U.S. Embassy in Mexico City and then in Tinian in the Marianas Islands. Following retirement, he was the Far East representative for the Isbrandsten Line. Crinkley died in Florida and was buried in Oakwood Cemetery in Raleigh.[163]

Then-Lieutenant Andrew Crinkley on board the USS *Langley*, circa 1923. *Naval History and Heritage Command.*

WILLIAM AUGUSTUS "WINNY" WINSTON (1896–1948) was born in Louisburg, Franklin County. He attended both Wake Forest and the University of North Carolina–Chapel Hill. In 1917, Winston joined the Army Signal Corps. Instead of heading overseas, he remained in the United States, where he taught other army aviators to fly. While stationed at Brooks Field, Texas, he taught Charles Lindbergh to fly. After leaving the army, Winston flew with the Philadelphia Transit Company and then became the national flying director of the Curtiss Flying Service. He joined Pan American Airways, where he logged over three million miles and became the first pilot to cross the Atlantic Ocean one hundred times. Winston was the pilot who flew the bodies of Will Rogers and Wiley Post back to the United States after their fatal plane crash in Alaska in 1935. He passed away in Coral Gables and was interred in the Arlington National Cemetery.[164]

Alton Stewart was the first licensed pilot in North Carolina. *North Carolina Museum of History.*

ALTON STEWART (1897–1929), born in Harnett County, was a mechanic and became the state's first licensed pilot. His license, no. 221, was signed by Orville Wright and issued in 1927. By 1926, he was reported as the best-known flier in the Southeast. Stewart also published the *Carolina Air News* and managed the Mashburn-Robbins Airfield in Raleigh. Stewart was killed in an accident in Dunn and is buried in the Coats City Cemetery.[165]

Frank Alton Armstrong Jr. (1902–1969) was born in Hamilton, Martin County. He graduated from Wake Forest College with a bachelor of science and law degree. Armstrong joined the Army Air Corps in 1928 and trained at Brooks Field and Kelly Field in Texas. After earning his wings and being commissioned into the army, he was posted to various assignments in Virginia, California, Texas, Louisiana and the Panama Canal. A combat observer in England, Armstrong later served as the assistant chief of air staff in Washington, D.C. Armstrong was one of the officers selected to go to England to establish the VIII Bomber Command. In July 1942, Armstrong assumed command of the 97th Bomb Group, training and then commanding the first U.S. Army Air Forces group to drop bombs on Occupied France. Later, Armstrong commanded the 306th Bomb Group, the first to drop bombs on Nazi Germany. This event became the basis for the novel and film *Twelve O'Clock High*, by Sy Bartlett and Beirne Lay Jr. Armstrong's promotion to brigadier general came in February 1943. He was assigned to command the 1st Bombardment Wing. After he was injured in a fire, Armstrong returned stateside. He held various commands thereafter and was considered to command the unit that dropped the atomic bomb. Instead, Armstrong was sent to Guam, where he commanded the 315th Bomb Wing. Armstrong's group made the final heavy bombing raid on Japan. His assignments as the chief of the staff of the Pacific Air Command, at the Armed Forces State College and as deputy commanding general of the Alaskan Air Command followed. Armstrong was promoted to lieutenant general and retired in July 1931. His son Major Frank A. Armstrong III was killed over Vietnam in 1967. Lieutenant General Armstrong was buried in Arlington National Cemetery.[166]

Mary Webb Nicholson (1905–1943), born in Greensboro, learned to fly while living in Ohio. Her license was granted in October 1929, and she returned to North Carolina. She was an original member of the Ninety-Nines and was appointed by Amelia Earhart as governor of the southeastern region. In May 1933, she earned her limited commercial pilot's license, followed by her transport license a year later. She was the first North Carolina woman to hold both licenses. Nicholson became Jackie Cochran's personal secretary in 1937, and when World War II began, she became one of the twenty-five women to join the British Air Transport Auxiliary to ferry planes from factories to Royal Air Force bases. She was killed in a crash just south of Birmingham, England, and was buried at New Garden Friends Cemetery in Greensboro. In 2022, she was inducted into the North Carolina Aviation Hall of Fame.[167]

Delmar Taft Spivey (1905–1982) was born in Gatesville. After graduating from high school in Virginia, he briefly attended William and Mary College before he was appointed to the U.S. Military Academy. A year after graduating in 1928, he attended flying school and was assigned to Langley Field, Virginia, after he completed the program. In 1936, Spivey became a flight instructor at Kelly Field, Texas, and then commanded a squadron at Eglin Field. In January 1941, Spivey was appointed executive officer of the Air Corps Proving Ground, Eglin Field. Colonel Spivey then commanded the Central Instructors School and Flexible Gunnery School at Buckingham Field in Fort Myers, Florida. Spivey, with another officer, developed the training procedures for gunners in bombers. While Spivey was serving with the Eighth Air Force in Europe, a B-17 Flying Fortress in which he was flying as an observer was shot down. Spivey became the highest-ranking prisoner of war in the European theater. On arriving at Stalag Luff III, Spivey was briefed by the other prisoners on the subversive activities of the camp. He even penned a secret history of the camp that he was able to smuggle out with him when he was sent on a mission by high-ranking SS officers who tried to end the war. Following World War II, Spivey held a number of important assignments, including as commander of the Japan Air Defense Force and commander of the Air War College. After his retirement at the grade of major general, Spivey spent a decade as the superintendent of a military school. He then retired to Florida. Spivey was buried at the U.S. Military Academy Post Cemetery in Orange County, New York.[168]

Albert "Al" Boyd (1906–1976) was born in Cocke County, Tennessee. His family returned to Asheville, where Boyd graduated from high school and attended Biltmore Junior College. Boyd was commissioned as a second lieutenant in the Army Air Corps in 1929 and served as a flying instructor in Texas. In 1934, he began serving as an engineering officer in Hawaii. During World War II, Boyd was stationed in Ohio and Pennsylvania. Over the next few years, General Boyd transferred to various commands, often testing new aircraft. In 1947, while flying a modified P-80 "Shooting Star," he set a world speed record. He was known as "the world's fastest general" and "the world's number one test pilot." It was Boyd who selected Chuck Yeager to pilot the X-1. Boyd logged more than twenty-three thousand flying hours and flew over seven hundred different variants or subvariants of aircraft.

At the time of his retirement, he was praised as the "Father of Modern Flight Testing" and the "Dean of American Test Pilots." Postretirement, he worked as the general manager of the defense division at Westinghouse Electric Corporation and as a test pilot with Lycoming Division, Avco. Boyd was buried in Arlington National Cemetery. A bridge over the French Broad River is named in his honor, and the P-80 of his record flight is on display in the National Museum of the U.S. Air Force.[169]

Effie Lucille Hogan Brockenbrough (1910–1985), born in Orange County, married Jim Brockenbrough in an open-cockpit plane. Jim was a barnstormer who flew around the country visiting airshows and giving flights. He taught her to fly, and she performed as a wing-walker. Lucille was also a member of the Ninety-Nines. The couple moved to Charlotte in 1936, where they sold Piper planes at the Douglas Airport. Later, they opened the Brockenbrough Airport on Statesville Road, where Lucille was a flight instructor and Civil Air Patrol commander. She and Jim were buried in the Huntersville Presbyterian Church Cemetery.[170]

Zachary Smith Reynolds (1911–1932) was born in Winston-Salem the son of R.J. Reynolds, the founder of the R.J. Reynolds Tobacco Company. He dropped out of high school to work at Reynolds Aviation in New York. In 1926, Reynolds started taking flying lessons, and he received his pilot license in August 1928. A year later, he received his transport pilot's license and his mechanic's license. All the while, he was traveling around North Carolina barnstorming at various airshows in a Waco 10 with a Whirlwind engine. In 1931, he purchased a Savoia-Marchetti biplane, and in December, he began a seventeen-thousand-mile journey from London to Chanchiang, China. Reynolds was found dead at his family home, Reynolda House, in Winston-Salem, on July 6, 1932. It is still unclear if his cause of death was suicide or murder. He was buried in the Salem Cemetery in Winston-Salem. In 2022, Reynolds was inducted into the North Carolina Aviation Hall of Fame.[171]

Dorothy "Dot" Swain Lewis (1915–2013), born near Asheville, graduated from Randolph-Macon Women's College in 1936 and then studied art at the New York Art Students League. In 1941, she earned her pilot's license and began working at Piper Aircraft in Lock Haven, Pennsylvania. Swain was trained as a flight instructor and earned her commercial pilot license. After training four classes of naval aviators, she joined the WASP program, where she trained pilots and flew bombers and fighters. She remained in the air force reserve until 1957. In the post–World War II years, Swain married Albert Z. Lewis, worked as the chief flight instructor at the airport in Daytona Beach and then moved to Arizona, where she taught at the Orme School. She was well known for creating a series of cast-bronze sculptures commemorating WASP pilots, along with many other artistic endeavors. Lewis moved to California and taught at the Idyllwild School of Music and the Arts. In 2010, she received the Congressional Gold Medal to commemorate the WASP's groundbreaking role in World War II.[172]

Dorothy "Dot" Post Hoover (1917–2015) was born in Buncombe County and graduated from Biltmore College in 1934. In 1938, she married Henry Hoover, and while living in Greenville, South Carolina, she volunteered for the Civilian Pilot Training Program at Furman University. After her husband was transferred overseas, Hoover, while working in Raleigh, saw an advertisement for women pilots. She wrote to Jackie Cochran and received orders to report to Sweetwater, Texas, for training. After graduation, Hoover trained glider pilots at South Plains Air Force Base in Lubbock, Texas; towed targets for aerial gunnery practice at Eagle Pass Air Force Base; and then taught at the Basic Instructor School in San Antonio. Following the war, she worked as a court reporter in Asheville. After her retirement, she penned over a dozen books. Hoover was buried at Lewis Memorial Park in Buncombe County.[173]

Katherine Stinson (1917–2001) was born in Fuquay-Varina and took her first flight at the age of ten. At fifteen, while working as a mechanic's assistant to raise money for flying lessons at the Raleigh Municipal Airport, she met Amelia Earhart. On learning that Stinson wanted to be a pilot, Earhart advised her to become an engineer instead. Stinson was the first woman to graduate from the engineering program at North Carolina State College. Her degree was in mechanical engineering with an aeronautics option. She worked for the Civil Aeronautics Administration, developing safety standards for airplanes. As the CAA became the Federal Aviation Administration, she continued to investigate crashes and modify faulty military aircraft designs. She also worked on standards for supersonic transportation. Stinson received the Sustained Superior Performance Award in 1961 and was a technical assistant in the Engineering and Manufacturing Division of the FAA from 1964 until her retirement in 1973.[174]

Thomas W. Ferebee (1918–2000) was born near Mocksville. He attended Lees McRae College in Avery County, lettering in track, basketball and football, and he planned to play Major League Baseball until an injury changed those plans. In the summer of 1941, Ferebee joined the Army Air Corps, and after flight training, he was trained as a bombardier. With the United States' entry into World War II, his B-17 flew sixty-three bombing missions over North Africa and Europe. In August 1944, Ferebee was

Katherine Stinson was the first woman to graduate from North Carolina State College with a degree in engineering. *State Archives of North Carolina.*

transferred to the 509th Composite Group, stationed at Wendover Field, Utah. Already considered the best bombardier in the United States, he honed his skills on dropping a large bomb from thirty thousand feet with pin-point accuracy. In May 1945, Ferebee was transferred to the island of Tinian, and on August 6, 1945, a B-29 named the *Enola Gay* took off bound for Japan. Once over Hiroshima, Ferebee dropped the first atomic bomb used in warfare. After the drop of a second atomic bomb a few days later, Japan surrendered, ending World War II. Ferebee remained in the military, flying B-52s in Vietnam. On retiring, he moved to Florida, where he sold real estate. He was inducted into the North Carolina Aviation Hall of Fame in 2022. Ferebee was buried in the Wesley Chapel United Methodist Church Cemetery in Mocksville.[175]

Thomas Henry Davis (1918–1999) was born in Winston-Salem. In 1934, he earned his pilot's license from the Camel City Flying Service and then his flight instructor's license. Davis was working as a salesman for Camel City Flying Service in 1939, and in 1940, he bought the company and changed its name to Piedmont Aviation Inc. During World War II, he trained over one thousand pilots in Winston-Salem and Greensboro. Following the war, Piedmont Airlines was created, with its first commercial flight in 1948. Davis became CEO of the company in 1981, and in 1983, he became chairman of the executive committee. He retired in 1984. Davis was honored with the Tony Jannus Award and the Daniel Guggenheim Medal. He was buried at Salem Cemetery in Forsyth County. In 2022, Davis was inducted into the North Carolina Aviation Hall of Fame.[176]

Robert Knight Morgan (1918–2004) was born in Asheville, attended the University of Pennsylvania and joined the Army Air Corps in 1940. On December 12, 1941, he was awarded his wings. After additional training, he was assigned to the 324th Bomb Squadron, 91st Bomb Group, piloting a B-17 Flying Fortress. His plane, the *Memphis Belle*, was the second bomber to complete twenty-five missions over Europe. Morgan and the crew flew the plane back to the States for a publicity tour. Morgan went on to command a B-29 Superfortress, the *Dauntless Dotty*, in the Pacific theater. In 1965, he retired from the air force as a colonel. He owned a Volkswagen dealership in Virginia and later returned to Asheville, where he penned his autobiography. He was inducted into the North Carolina Aviation Hall of Fame in 2022. Morgan was buried at the Western Carolina Veterans Cemetery in Swannanoa.[177]

Kate Lee Harris Adams (1919–2002) was born in Durham. While studying at Duke University, she was able to join the Civil Pilot Training Program. After graduation from Duke, she attempted to join the WASP program but did not have enough flying hours. Later, when the program reduced the number of hours a pilot needed, she was able to join. As a WASP, she ferried planes from Napier Field in Alabama to other airbases across the United States and served as a flight instructor. She met her husband at Napier Field. After the war, they moved to Texas. When her

Above, left: Davie County native Thomas W. Ferebee (*right*) is awarded the Distinguished Flying Cross by Brigadier General Joseph A. Atkinson. *National Archives.*

Above, right: Asheville native Robert Morgan piloted the *Memphis Belle* on twenty-five bombing runs over Europe. *National Archives.*

Left: Durham native Kate Lee Harris Adams served in the Women Air Service Pilots (WASP) during World War II. *Texas Women's University.*

husband died, Kate moved back to Durham and was instrumental in the WASP finally receiving credit for their World War II achievements. She was buried in Maplewood Cemetery, Durham.[178]

Willie Howard Fuller (1919–1995) was born in Tarboro. He attended local schools and graduated from Tuskegee Institute with a bachelor's degree in mechanical industries in 1942. After graduating from the Tuskegee Advanced Pilot cadet program, he was commissioned a second lieutenant and earned his wings. During World War II, he flew seventy-six combat missions over Sicily and Italy with the Ninety-Ninth Fighter Squadron. On his return to the United States, Fuller became the first Black flight instructor in advanced single-engine airplanes at Tuskegee Army Air Field. After his discharge in 1947, Fuller served in the U.S. Air Force Reserves. He trained pilots in Tarboro and then moved to LaGrange, Georgia, where he owned a taxicab company. He then moved to Miami, Florida, where he served as the district executive with the Boy Scouts of America. Fuller was buried in Dade Memorial Park in Opa-locka, Florida.[179]

GEORGE E. PREDDY JR. (1919–1944) was born in Greensboro and attended Guilford College for two years. In early 1939, he soloed and, along with local aviator Bill Teague, purchased an airplane and began barnstorming and taking passengers up for rides on the weekends. The U.S. Navy rejected him as an aviator three times due to his high blood pressure and a curvature of the spine. A few months later, he was accepted in the U.S. Army Air Corps. Five days after the attack on Pearl Harbor, he was awarded his pilot's wings. Preddy first served in Australia, where he downed two Japanese fighters before he was wounded in a midair collision. After recovering, he was assigned to the 487th Fighter Squadron, 352nd Fighter Group, and was stationed in England. Over the next sixteen months, he flew 143 combat missions, with 26.83 aerial victories. Preddy was killed in a friendly fire episode on Christmas Day 1944. He was the third-highest ace of the European theater during World War II and ranked seventh of all U.S. aces. In 2022, Preddy was inducted into the North Carolina Aviation Hall of Fame.[180]

Vernon Haywood was born in Raleigh and flew with the Tuskegee Airmen. *North Carolina Museum of History.*

VERNON V. HAYWOOD (1920–2003) was born in Raleigh. After graduating from high school in 1938, he attended Hampton University, where he enrolled in the Civilian Pilot Training Program. Haywood then went to Tuskegee Army Air Field for fighter pilot training. As a pilot in the Army Air Corps, Haywood spent fifteen months escorting bombers to their targets in Europe. He was commander of the 302nd Fighter Squadron. After seventy missions, he returned to the United States. He became the Tuskegee Air Field Instrument

School's Assistant Director, and then in 1949, Haywood became one of the first four Black jet flight instructors in the U.S. Air Force at Williams Air Force Base in Arizona. He went on to serve in various roles in Japan, the Philippines and Vietnam. After logging more than six thousand flight hours, he retired with the rank of colonel in 1971. Haywood was interred at Arlington National Cemetery.[181]

Harold Kimball "Zeke" Saunders (1921–2014) was born in Catawba County. After learning to fly at the age of seventeen, Saunders worked at the airport in Martindale, Virginia. He was hired by Tom Davis as a flight instructor for the Civilian Pilot Training Program at Smith Reynolds Airport. In 1944, Saunders joined the U.S. Army Air Forces, flying transport planes in the China-Burma-India theater of the Pacific war. One of his missions at the end of the war was to bring home survivors from the Bataan Death March. Saunders returned to Piedmont Airlines after his military service, where he occupied a variety of positions, including chief pilot, director of operations, vice president of operations and chair on the board of directors. Saunders retired in 1984. He was interred at the Olivet Baptist Church Cemetery in Catawba County. In 2022, Saunders was inducted into the North Carolina Aviation Hall of Fame.[182]

Johnny O. "Jocko" Crowell (1922–1989) was born in Charlotte. His father, John Edison Crowell, was a barnstormer and airshow pilot. After graduating from Charlotte Technical High School, he joined the Army Air Corps. Crowell was assigned to the 390th Fighter Squadron, 366th Fighter Group, in Europe. Following his service overseas, Crowell enlisted in the North Carolina Air National Guard. According to his obituary, Crowell was the first pilot sworn into the 156th Fighter Squadron, North Carolina Air National Guard, when it was federalized for service in the Korean War. Lieutenant Colonel Crowell retired from the U.S. Air Force in 1966. From Charlotte, he operated Crowell Aero Service, checking on power lines, pulling aerial banners and, during protests in North and South Carolina over the Vietnam War, pulling a large American flag with his J-3 Cub. Crowell was inducted into the OX-5 Aviation Hall of Fame. He was buried at Sharon Memorial Park in Mecklenburg County.[183]

Thomas "Tom" Oxendine (1922–2010) was born in Robeson County and graduated from the Cherokee Indian Normal School at the age of fifteen. While attending the Cherokee Normal College (now the University of North Carolina at Pembroke), he began taking flight classes, earning his pilot's license three months later. Natives were not allowed to become officers at the time. Due to the wartime need for aviators, an exception was made, and Oxendine became the first Native to earn his naval aviator wings without being a graduate of the Naval Academy. He served in three different conflicts: World War II, Korea and Vietnam. And he earned the Distinguished Flying Cross for rescuing a downed airman in 1944 off Yap Island, Japan. Oxendine also served as a test pilot for carrier-based aircraft and as a flight instructor. After twenty-nine years, he retired from the navy at the rank of commander. He then served for sixteen years as the chief of public affairs for the Bureau of Indian Affairs in Washington, D.C., and then another fifteen years as a consultant for American Indians and Alaska Natives with a consulting group in Washington, D.C. His other honors include being the first Distinguished Alumnus of UNC-Pembroke, being inducted into the first Athletic Hall of Fame class at the university and being one of North Carolina's "Famous Tar Heels." Oxendine passed away in Arlington and was buried in Sandcutt Cemetery, Robeson County.[184]

Conrad Selwyn "Gus" Shinn (1922) was born in Spray, Rockingham County. After graduating as valedictorian from high school, he attended Lees-McRae College and North Carolina State University. Shinn participated in the Civilian Pilot Training Program at the Raleigh Municipal Airport and, after joining the navy, enrolled in preflight training at the University of North Carolina. After earning his wings, he was stationed in the Pacific theater during World War II. There, he flew supplies, wounded men and repatriated prisoners in and out of the area. After the war, Shinn was one of the pilots selected for Operation Highjump, which established an Antarctic research base. After this assignment, he spent the next few years ferrying naval brass; then he served in Naval Training Command in Pensacola and piloted helicopters on antisubmarine patrols off the coasts of Florida and North Carolina. In 1955, Shinn was selected for a trip to the South Pole, part of an International Geophysical Year program. A specially equipped R4D-5, piloted by Shinn, became the first airplane to land on the South Pole on October 31, 1956. A base was established, and Shinn made five additional flights over the next four months. Shinn retired from the navy as a lieutenant commander. Mount Shinn, near the Ellsworth Mountains in Antarctica, is named for him. In 2023, a mural to Shinn was dedicated in Eden, North Carolina.[185]

John Anderson McGlohon (1923–2020) was born in Guilford County and moved to Randolph County as an infant. At the age of eighteen, in June 1941, he enlisted in the Army Air Corps. McGlohon was trained as an aerial photographer, assigned to the 3rd Photographic Reconnaissance Squadron. During World War II, McGlohon photographed and mapped

South America, Alaska, China, Burma and India. In August 1945, his plane photographed the atomic bomb the *Enola Gay* dropped on Hiroshima. Following the war, he returned to Asheboro, worked for the U.S. Postal Service, ran a photography studio, sold auto parts and eventually served as the fire chief for the City of Asheboro. His brother Robert died in a crash in England while serving in the 511th Bomber Squadron, 351st Bomber Group. John A. McGlohon was buried in Oaklawn Cemetery, Randolph County.[186]

Myrtle "Kay" Thompson Cagle (1925–2019) was born in Sanford and taught to fly at a young age by her brother. At the age of fourteen, she became the youngest licensed pilot in the state. When the aviation instructor at her high school was drafted, Cagle took over. She joined the Civil Air Patrol and the Ninety-Nines, and at the age of eighteen, she attempted to join the WASP, but she did not meet the height requirements. She went on to receive her private and commercial licenses and purchased her own plane, all before the age of twenty-three. In 1946, she began writing an aviation column for the *Johnstonian Sun*. It was later picked up by the *Raleigh News and Observer*. In 1952, she opened a flying school in Selma and then became one of the first women to pilot a jet. She married Walt Cagle in 1960, and the couple moved to Macon, Georgia. On learning of the program that was "training" women to be astronauts, Cagle wrote and gained entrance to the program. With twelve others, she went through a battery of tests to see if women could pass the same tests as those administered to the Mercury astronauts. Often, the women, known now as the Mercury 13, passed with better results than the men. However, the program never gained NASA approval and, despite congressional hearings, was canceled. Cagle returned to Macon and taught students to fly. In 2003, she was inducted into the Georgia Aviation Hall of Fame and was honored with an honorary doctorate from the University of Wisconsin–Oshkosh in 2007, along with eight other Mercury 13 women. Cagle passed away in 2019.[187]

Sam Beddingfield (1933–2012) was born in Clayton and graduated from North Carolina State University in 1956 with a degree in aeronautical engineering. He joined the air force and served as a test pilot at Wright-Patterson Air Force Base in Ohio. He developed a friendship with Gus Grissom. After Beddingfield left the air force, he was able to land a job at the fledgling NASA in October 1959. Beddingfield oversaw the mechanical and pyrotechnic systems of the Mercury capsule. Later, he worked on the Gemini and Apollo programs, and he was the first engineer to switch from the Apollo to the Space Shuttle program. Beddingfield retired as the deputy director of Shuttle Operations in 1985. He was a frequent commentator on shuttle launches and volunteered at the U.S. Space Walk of Fame Foundation and the Valiant Air Command Warbird Museum. Beddingfield passed away in Titusville, Florida.[188]

Ruby L. (Campbell) Bostic (1933) was born in Chadbourn, Columbus County. She graduated from Chadbourne High School, St. Augustine's College and Adelphi University. She moved to New York after getting married in 1955, and in 1978, she received her pilot's license. On February 10, 1985, Ruby and a fellow pilot, Melva Jackman, took off from New York for Trinidad and Tobago in a Piper Cherokee and arrived on February 14. They became the first Black women to fly a single-engine plane from New York to Trinidad, earning a spot in the *Guinness Book of World Records*. Ruby is a member of many organizations, including the Ninety-Nines, the Falcon Squadron of the Civil Air Patrol and the Claude B. Govan Tri-State Chapter of the Tuskegee Airmen.[189]

Charles "Charlie" Duke Jr. (1935) was born in Charlotte, where his father was working as an insurance salesman. Following the United States' entrance into World War II, his father joined the navy, and the family moved to California. Once Charlie's father was deployed overseas, the family moved to Johnston, South Carolina. After World War II ended, the family settled in Lancaster, South Carolina. Duke was admitted to the U.S. Naval Academy but switched to the new U.S. Air Force Academy, where he graduated in 1957. After flight training in various aircraft and at various bases, Duke was sent to West Germany. Three years later, he was stateside again, where he earned a master of science degree in aeronautics and astronautics at the Massachusetts Institute of Technology. He then attended the Aerospace Research Pilot School at Edwards Air Force Base, where he tied for second in his class. After graduation, he instructed students in various fighter jets. It was announced in April 1966 that Duke was a member of the fifth group of NASA astronauts. After astronaut training, Duke was CAPCOM for *Apollo 10* and *Apollo 11* and a part of the backup crew for *Apollo 13*. Duke served as lunar module pilot for *Apollo 16* and spent several days on the

Charlie Duke, lunar module pilot of *Apollo 16*, was one of the twelve men who walked on the Moon. *NASA*.

lunar surface in April 1972. Duke retired from NASA in 1976 but continued to serve in the air force reserve until 1986, when he retired as a brigadier general. In 1983, he was inducted into the U.S. Astronaut Hall of Fame, and in 2022, he was inducted into the North Carolina Aviation Hall of Fame. He and his wife, Dorothy, now live in Texas, and they coauthored *Moon Walker* in 1990.[190]

Richard Ritchie was one of the five United States Vietnam War combat aces. *United States Air Force.*

Richard Stephen Ritchie (1942) was born in Reidsville. After graduating from the U.S. Air Force Academy in 1964 with a bachelor of science degree in engineering, he was assigned to Eglin Air Force Base in Florida, where he flew F-104 Starfighters, and later, while stationed at Homestead Air Force Base in Florida, he flew F-4 Phantom IIs. In 1968, Ritchie was assigned to the 480th Tactical Fighter Squadron, 366th Tactical Fighter Wing, stationed at Da Nang Air Base in South Vietnam. After returning to the States in 1969, while stationed at Nellis Air Force Base in Nevada, he became the youngest Air Force Fighter Weapons School instructor. Ritchie returned for a second tour in Vietnam in 1972. He was assigned to the 555th Tactical Fighter Squadron, 432nd Tactical Reconnaissance Wing, at Udorn Royal Thai Air Force Base in Thailand. During this tour, Ritchie shot down five enemy jets, making him one of five U.S. aces of the Vietnam War and one of the most decorated. He earned the 1972 Mackay Trophy, the 1972 Jabara Award and the 1972 Armed Forces Award. In 1974, Ritchie left active duty, joined the air national guard, ran for Congress from North Carolina, worked for the Adolph Coors Company and later joined the Colorado National Guard. He was promoted to brigadier general in the air force reserve in 1994 and retired in 1995. Ritchie now lives in Colorado and is a motivational speaker.[191]

William "Warren" Hervey Wheeler (1943) was born in Durham and attended North Carolina Agricultural and Technical College for a year. Wheeler earned his commercial pilot's license from the American Flyers School in Ardmore, Oklahoma. He returned to North Carolina in 1962 and opened his own flight school and charter service at Horace Williams Airport in Chapel Hill. Wheeler became the first Black pilot for Piedmont Airlines in 1966, and three years later, he founded the Wheeler Flying

Service, later known as Wheeler Airlines, the first airline opened by a Black American. Although the company eventually closed, Wheeler continued to fly for a number of years for USAir and served on the board of directors of Opportunity Skyway before he retired in 1995. In 2022, Wheeler was inducted into the North Carolina Aviation Hall of Fame.[192]

Michael John Smith (1945–1986) was born in Beaufort. After he graduated from East Carteret High School, he entered the U.S. Naval Academy and graduated in 1967. He then earned a master of science degree from the U.S. Naval Postgraduate School. In 1969, he earned his wings, served as an instructor and completed a tour in Vietnam flying A-6 Intruders. Smith then completed test pilot school, worked on missile guidance systems, served as an instructor and completed two tours on the USS *Saratoga* in the Mediterranean. In May 1980, Smith was selected for the astronaut program. He served in various administrative roles before he was chosen as the pilot of the *Challenger* for STS-61-A. *Challenger* disintegrated during its launch on January 28, 1986, killing the entire crew. In 2022, Smith was inducted into the North Carolina Aviation Hall of Fame.[193]

NASA astronaut and Beaufort native Michael J. Smith was killed in the Space Shuttle *Challenger* explosion in 1986. *NASA*.

William Surles McArthur Jr. (1951) was born in Laurinburg. He graduated from the U.S. Military Academy in 1973 with a degree in applied science and engineering. McArthur served with the Eighty-Second Airborne Division and attended the U.S. Army Aviation School. He then earned a master of science degree in aerospace engineering from Georgia Institute of Technology in 1983. In 1987, he attended the U.S. Naval Test Pilot School, and in 1990, he was selected as an astronaut. McArthur flew on STS-58 in 1993; STS-74 in 1995 and STS-92 in 2000. From October 3, 2005, to April 8, 2006, McArthur was stationed on the International Space Station, a part of Expedition 12. The Russian Soyuz capsule was his ride on that mission. He went on to serve as the director of safety and mission assurance at Johnson Space Flight Center until his retirement in 2017.[194]

Charles E. Brady Jr. (1951–2006) was born in Pinehurst. He studied pre-med at the University of North Carolina–Chapel Hill and graduated in 1971, and then he received a medical degree from Duke University in 1975.

After joining the U.S. Navy in 1986, he was trained as a flight surgeon and assigned to the USS *Ranger*. From 1988 to 1990, Brady was flight surgeon for the Blue Angels. Brady was selected for the astronaut program in 1992 and served as a mission specialist on STS-78 in 1996. He retired from the navy in 2006. Brady was interred in the Prosperity Friends Meeting Cemetery in Moore County.[195]

Ellen Louise Shulman Baker (1953) was born in Fayetteville. She has degrees from the University of Buffalo and Cornell University and earned a doctorate in medicine from the University of Texas School of Public Health. Baker first served as a medical officer for NASA and was selected as an astronaut in June 1985. She served as a mission specialist on three space shuttle missions: STS-34 in 1989, STS-50 in 1992, and STS-71 in 1995. Following these missions, Baker served as chief of the Astronaut Office Education/Medical Branch, retiring in 2011.[196]

Curtis Lee "Curt" Brown (1955) was born in Elizabethtown. He graduated from the U.S. Air Force Academy in 1978 and completed pilot training in July 1979. Brown flew A-10s and completed test pilot school. In June 1987, he was selected as an astronaut candidate, going on to serve on six space flights: STS-47 in 1992, STS-66 in 1994, STS-77 in 1996, STS-85 in 1997, STS-95 in 1998 and STS-103 in 1999. Brown retired from NASA in May 2000 and went on to become a pilot for American Airlines and Sun Country Airlines. In 2010, Brown was inducted into the U.S. Astronaut Hall of Fame.[197]

Susan Jane Helms (1958) was born in Charlotte, North Carolina. She graduated with a bachelor of science degree in aeronautical engineering from the U.S. Air Force Academy in 1980, a master of science degree from Stanford University in 1985 and from the U.S. Air Force Test Pilot School in 1988. She participated in four shuttle missions: STS-54 in 1993, STS-64 in 1994, STS-78 in 1996 and STS-101 in 2000. Helms was also a member of the International Space Station's Expedition 2 crew in 2001. She logged over five thousand hours in space, including a world record EVA of eight hours and fifty-six minutes. Helms retired from the U.S. Air Force in 2014 at the rank of lieutenant general. She was inducted into the U.S. Astronaut Hall of Fame in 2011.[198]

Thomas Henry Marshburn (1960) was born in Statesville. He earned degrees in physics from Davidson College in 1982, engineering physics from the University of Virginia in 1984, medicine from Wake Forest University in 1989 and medical science from the University of Texas Medical Branch in 1997. In 1994, Marshburn joined NASA, serving as a flight surgeon at

Johnson Space Center, and he was involved with various missions, including as the cochair of medical operations for the Shuttle-Mir Program. He was also the medical operations lead for the International Space Station. In 2004, Marshburn was selected to be an astronaut. He served on STS-127 in 2009 Expedition 34/35 on the International Space Station and SpaceX Crew-3, taking over command of the International Space Station in 2022. He retired from NASA and took a position as the chief medical officer at Sierra Space.[199]

ROBERT "FARMER" HINES (1975) was born in Fayetteville. He graduated from Boston University with a bachelor of science degree in aerospace engineering. Hines then joined the U.S. Air Force and graduated from the Air Force Officer Training School and then pilot training in 2000. His additional training was conducted at Seymour Johnson Air Force Base, followed by a tour in the Middle East. Hines attended the U.S. Air Force Test Pilot School, where he received a master of science degree in flight test engineering and then later earned a master of science degree in aerospace engineering at the University of Alabama. Among his many assignments was that as a test pilot at Johnson Space Center. His selection as an astronaut came in 2017. Hines was the pilot of SpaceX Crew-4 in 2022.[200]

8
SOME OF NORTH CAROLINA'S AVIATION TRAGEDIES

With the trial and error of heavier-than-air flight pioneered by the Wright brothers at Kitty Hawk, they of course deserve the first mention of an airplane crash. From the first accidents that wrecked the original *Wright Flyer*, the history of flight is one fraught with danger. According to the Bureau of Aircraft Accidents Archives, there have been 158 aircraft accidents in North Carolina, with a total of 736 fatalities. Considering how often these early aircraft "broke up" during exhibitions and demonstrations, these numbers probably do not represent the actual incidents. The following is a list of some of the more notable and tragic crashes within North Carolina.

HATTERAS: On March 5, 1942, a B-17 Flying Fortress took off from Langley Field, Virginia, on a routine patrol over the Atlantic Ocean. Its last reported position was off Cape Hatteras, at 11:00 a.m. After an extensive search produced no trace of the bomber, the eight-man crew was declared missing and assumed lost at sea.[201]

ALBEMARLE SOUND: On March 30, 1943, a Consolidated PBY Catalina, flying low over the Albemarle Sound, had a wing hit the water. The plane water-looped and sank. All eight servicemen on board were killed.[202]

BURKE COUNTY: On May 15, 1943, a Douglas C-47 Skytrain left Laurinburg-Maxton Army Air Base with eighteen on board. The passengers were being

This memorial commemorates the lives of the eighteen Army Air Forces pilots killed in a crash in 1943 on Gingercake Mountain. *Author's collection.*

trained as glider pilots for the Normandy invasion. A little after 4:30 p.m., the plane, while flying through fog, slammed into Gingercake Mountain in Burke County. All eighteen on board were killed.[203]

Maxton AFB: On June 7, 1943, a C-47 with four crew and sixteen glider pilots took off from Pope Field. The plane encountered a thunderstorm and went down within sight of the Laurinburg-Maxton Army Air Field, killing all aboard.[204]

Maxton AFB: On September 20, 1943, a Douglas C-53 Skytrooper took off from Laurinburg-Maxton Airport. The airplane, with twenty-five servicemen, "whipstalled" and crashed in a swamp only a half a mile from the runway. All on board were killed.[205]

Mackall AAFB: A Douglas C-47 Skytrain, with eighteen on board, lost its engine(s) while landing on October 29, 1943. The plane clipped trees and crashed near the runway. Fourteen were killed.

Hertford: A Martin PGM Mariner on a training mission crashed on May 31, 1944, in the Harvey Point Naval Auxiliary Air Station, killing all nine on board.[206]

Mackall AFF: Eight paratroopers and four crewmen were killed when their C-47 crashed during a nighttime mass parachute jump on September 24, 1944. Four paratroopers were able to leap to safety.[207]

McDowell County: On June 13, 1944, a B-24 bomber on training mission from Chatham Field, Savannah, Georgia, slammed into Green Knob a half mile south of the Blue Ridge Parkway. All ten airmen on board were killed.[208]

Cold Mountain: On September 13, 1946, a B-25 bomber, while flying from Detroit to MacDill Air Field in Tampa, Florida, crashed into Cold Mountain in Haywood County. Among the five killed were Major General Paul Wurtsmith, the commander of the Eighth Air Force, Strategic Air Command.[209]

Mt. Mitchell: A Douglas C-47 Skytrain from Bolling Air Force Base, bound for Brookley Air Force Base, crashed into Mt. Mitchell on February 5, 1949. It took two days for anyone to find the wreckage. All nine on board were killed.[210]

Pope AFB: During a parachute training drop at Fort Bragg on November 17, 1953, a Fairchild C-119 Flying Boxcar experienced a malfunction, broke formation and crashed, killing eight on board. On the way down, seven paratroopers, dangling under their parachutes, were also killed by the C-119.[211]

Bolivia: On January 6, 1960, National Airlines Flight 2511, a Douglas DC-6 en route from New York to Miami, exploded midair near Bolivia, New Hanover County, killing all thirty-four people aboard. Among those lost was retired U.S. Navy Vice Admiral Edward O. McDonnell, a veteran of both World Wars and a Medal of Honor recipient. Investigations concluded that a bomb made of dynamite was to blame. No one was ever charged with or claimed responsibility for this act of terrorism, although the case remains unsolved.[212]

Hendersonville: On July 19, 1967, Piedmont Airlines flight PIO22 took off from Asheville Regional Airport. Three minutes later, while climbing to its assigned altitude, the Boeing 727 collided with a Cessna 310. All eighty-two occupants of both aircraft were killed. Limited visibility due to cloud cover was blamed for the crash.[213]

Silk Hope: A Douglas C-47 Skytrain involved in a training mission from Fort Bragg was carrying eleven members of the U.S. Army Parachute Team Golden Knights when it crashed in a field on March 8, 1973, near Silk Hope, Chatham County. All fourteen occupants were killed. Later investigations concluded that a reinforced floor that was not logged had led to the plane being overweight.[214]

Charlotte: Eastern Airlines Flight 212, a McDonnell Douglas DC9, was on the way from Charleston to Chicago, with a stop in Charlotte. Due to a dense fog on the morning of September 11, 1974, the plane was forced to make an instrument approach. Three miles from the runway, the jet was too low and clipped some trees. Seventy-two of the eighty-two passengers on board were killed or later died of their injuries. The National Transportation Safety Board later ruled that the members of the flight crew were distracted, leading to the crash.[215]

Raleigh-Durham: On February 19, 1988, American Eagle Flight 3378 crashed near a reservoir shortly after takeoff, killing all twelve people on board. The Swearingen SA227 Metro III was bound for Richmond, Virginia. The National Transportation Safety Board later ruled that the crew was not properly trained, and they failed to maintain a proper flight path.[216]

Pope AFB: On March 23, 1994, a Lockheed C-130E approached the landing strip at Pope Air Force Base. A U.S. Air Force F-16 was on the same approach when it and the C-130 collided. The C-130 was able to land safely. The pilots of the F-16 ejected to safety. The F-16 then crashed into a C-141 Starlifter that was sitting on the ground. There were around five hundred paratroopers nearby being loaded onto the C-141. Twenty-three paratroopers who were already on board were killed, and eighty others were wounded.[217]

Charlotte: USAir Flight 1016 originated in Columbia, South Carolina, and while it was attempting to land in Charlottle, it crashed into a house. Of the fifty-seven on board, thirty-seven were killed on July 2, 1994. Rain and a micro-induced windshear, with a lack of information regarding the weather from the tower, were listed as the causes of the crash.[218]

Raleigh: American Eagle Flight 3379, a BAe Jetstream 31 traveling between Greensboro and Raleigh with eighteen people on board, experienced engine problems. As the pilot attempted to land, the airplane struck some trees and crashed about four miles northwest of the runway. Thirteen of the eighteen people on board were killed in the crash on December 13, 1994.[219]

Charlotte: On January 8, 2003, a Beechcraft 1900D, USAir Flight 5481, that was headed to Greenville-Spartanburg crashed into the airport hangar during takeoff. All twenty-one passengers and crew on board were killed. Maintenance issues were listed as the cause of the crash.[220]

9

LOOKING FOR NORTH CAROLINA'S AVIATION HERITAGE

MUSEUMS AND STATIC DISPLAYS

Across the state, there are museums dedicated to the history of aviation as well as a number of static display aircraft preserved as historic artifacts. Visiting these sites is a wonderful way to learn more of the aviation history of the Old North State.

ASHEBORO

North Carolina Aviation Museum and Hall of Fame

In 1996, Asheboro businessman Jim Peddycorn formed the Foundation for Aircraft Conservation. That year, the foundation held its first airshow at the Asheboro Regional Airport. Peddycorn was killed in a crash not long thereafter, and the museum became the Peddycorn Foundation for Aircraft Conservation. In 2001, the general assembly designated the museum as the North Carolina Aviation Hall of Fame, and the name of the museum was changed to the North Carolina Aviation Museum and Hall of Fame. In two hangars, the museum has an impressive collection of aircraft, vehicles and artifacts. There are numerous displays, including ones on World War II fighter ace Major George E. Preddy Jr., Piedmont Airlines and important local aviation events.

Top: In 2024, the *Spirit of North Carolina*, a B-26 Invader, underwent restoration at the North Carolina Aviation Museum and Hall of Fame. *Author's collection.*

Bottom: This replica P-40, a monument to World War II aviator Lieutenant Robert Upchurch, is on display at the Carthage Community Airfield. *Author's collection.*

Carthage

James Rogers McConnell Air Museum

North Carolina's newest aviation museum, the James Rogers McConnell Air Museum, opened in 2023. The museum features several aircraft, models,

U.S. Airmail beacons and information on local fliers, including the museum's namesake, World War I aviator James R. McConnell. Outside, visitors can find a Vietnam-era Grumman OV-1 Mohawk.

CHARLOTTE

Sullenberger Aviation Museum

Formerly known as the Carolina Aviation Museum, which was founded in 1992, the Sullenberger Aviation Museum reopened after a lengthy renovation in June 2024. While there are over fifty aircraft located inside and outside the new hangar, the most famous is U.S. Airways Flight 1549, the "Miracle on the Hudson." Bound for Charlotte on January 15, 2009, this Airbus A320 was forced to land in the Hudson River not long after takeoff, as it ran into a flight of geese that knocked out both engines. The pilot, Chesley "Sully" Sullenberger, was able to save all of the passengers and crew. The Sullenberger Aviation Museum features many hands-on and STEM activities for children. Also on the grounds is the museum's original building, constructed by the Works Progress Administration in 1932.

FAYETTEVILLE

Airborne & Special Operations Museum

The history of the U.S. Army's airborne troops is told in fascinating detail at the Airborne & Special Operations Museum. Much of that history focuses on the World War II era, when airborne operations commenced. There are several aircraft on display, including a Waco CG-4A Hadrian Glider and a C-47A Skytrain. Later airborne operations are also explored with aircraft like a Bell UH-1H Iroquois helicopter and a Hughes MH-6C Cayuse helicopter. This museum opened in 2000.

A C6-4A Waco Glider can be seen unloading vehicles at the U.S. Army Airborne and Special Operations Museum in Fayetteville. *Author's collection.*

Fort Fisher

North Carolina Military History Museum

Located at the Blakeslee Air Force Recreation Area, not far from Fort Fisher, the North Carolina Military History Museum tells the story of North Carolina's military forces. The museum includes a Bell UH-1 Iroquois helicopter on display outside, along with various tanks, artillery pieces and antiaircraft guns.

Havelock

Havelock Tourist and Event Center

Numerous displays on local history, not just aviation, inform visitors of the importance of the area. The museum, located at the Havelock Tourist and Event Center, was established by Eastern Carolina Aviation Heritage Foundation in 2002. Much of the local history focuses on the Marine Corps Air Station Cherry Point. There are several aircraft outside, with a simulator and various displays and model aircraft inside. There are also displays on local history, including railroads and the Civil War era.

Hendersonville

Western North Carolina Air Museum

Founded in 1989, the Western North Carolina Air Museum is the oldest aviation museum in the state. Located at the Hendersonville Airport, the museum features twenty-three aircraft, simulators, a large library of reference material and various pieces of memorabilia. There is even a restoration area where various projects are undergoing repair and refurbishment. President George H.W. Bush visited the museum during a campaign stop in September 1992, and he checked out a Stearman N2S-4, the same type of aircraft in which he learned to fly during World War II.

The Western North Carolina Air Museum in Hendersonville is the oldest aviation museum in North Carolina. *Author's collection.*

Hickory

Hickory Aviation Museum

Located at the Hickory Regional Airport, the museum began as a group formed in 1991 to restore a North American FJ-3 Fury on display in Taylorsville. The group was known as the Sabre Society and moved the old aircraft to Hickory. The Hickory Aviation Museum had its grand opening in May 2007. The museum has an impressive collection of aircraft, including the only surviving Curtiss XF15C, a prototype mixed-propulsion fighter developed in the 1940s. The museum also has the only surviving P-80 Shooting Star that was used by the U.S. Navy, along with a Lockheed P-3C Orion that is open for tours. In 2022, it was announced that, in conjunction with the Catawba Valley Community College, a new building was being constructed to house the museum.

Kill Devil Hills

Wright Brothers National Memorial Park

Orville and Wilbur Wright would scarcely recognize the place where they perfected their gliders and first flew in the early 1900s. Orville Wright, along with Amelia Earhart, was present when the stone monument with a bronze plaque was dedicated in 1928 to commemorate the first flight.

The Wright brothers and their famous flight are commemorated with several memorials, including this bronze *Wright Flyer*. *Author's collection.*

The granite monument atop Kill Devil Hills was dedicated in 1932, with Orville Wright and Ruth Nichols attending. The current visitor center was dedicated on December 17, 1960, and due to its pioneering modernist design, it was placed on the National Register of Historic Places in 1975. In December 2003, the Centennial of Flight was celebrated, with appearances by President George W. Bush, astronauts Neil Armstrong and Buzz Aldrin and test pilot Chuck Yeager. Visitors today will find a replica of the *Wright Flyer* in the visitor center, monuments, reconstructions of the sheds in which the Wright brothers lived while they worked on their *Flyer* and a full-size bronze replica of the 1903 *Wright Flyer* at the moment of flight.

MANTEO

Dare County Regional Airport Museum

Located in the terminal building at the Dare County Airport, this museum picks up the story of local aviation after the Wright brothers' first flight. A large part of that story comes from War World II, when the Civil Air Patrol established a base at nearby Skyco Airport. Midway through the war, the base was moved to the current airport's location. There are model airplanes, information on local aviator Dave Driskell and World War II gear. Outside, there is a monument to the members of the local World War II Civil Air Patrol base.

SPENCER

North Carolina Transportation Museum

Located in the old Southern Railroad Company's largest steam locomotive servicing center, the North Carolina Transportation Museum not only houses an impressive display of locomotives and rolling stock, but it also includes displays on aviation. From its *Wright Flyer* to a large exhibit on Piedmont Airlines, the museum does not overlook air transportation history in North Carolina. The museum has a Piedmont Airlines DC-3 undergoing restoration. The North Carolina Transportation Museum was birthed in 1977, when the Southern Railway donated four acres to the state of North Carolina. The first exhibit was opened in 1983.

Outdoor Static Displays

Across North Carolina, there are numerous outdoor static displays of aircraft that are not directly tied to public museums. Many of these are located on military bases, and while they are available for public viewing, they may not always be accessible. Visitors are advised to always follow the directions and, when on a military base, please adhere to all the rules.

BEAUFORT

Marine Corps Air Station, Merritt Field

- North American FJ-3 Fury

BESSEMER CITY

City Park

- Lockheed F-94C Starfire

CAMP MACKALL, RICHMOND AND SCOTLAND COUNITES

- glider, monument off Ashemore Road

CANDLER

Enka Junior High School

- Republic RF-84F Thunderstreak

CARTHAGE

Gillam-McConnell Airfield

A Curtiss P-40 Warhawk replica is on display at the Carthage, North Carolina community airfield. This aircraft is part of a monument to Lieutenant Robert Hoyle Upchurch, who was a citizen of Carthage in Moore County, North Carolina. He was a fighter pilot with the Flying Tigers in World War II and was reported missing in action (MIA) in 1944. Years later, his remains were found and identified, and in 2006, they were returned to Carthage.

CHARLOTTE

Charlotte-Douglas International Airport, North Carolina Air National Guard

- Lockheed C-130B Hercules
- North American F-86L Sabre Dog

CLINTON

North Carolina Army National Guard Facility

- Bell UH-1C Iroquois helicopter

ELIZABETH CITY

Coast Guard Air Station

- Grumman HU-16E Albatross
- Sikorsky HH-52A Seaguard helicopter

FAYETTEVILLE

Eighty-Second Airborne Division War Memorial Museum

The Hall of Heroes and gift shop are open limited hours, but there is an excellent collection of aircraft on display outdoors. Since the site is included in Fort Liberty (Bragg), access is limited.

- Bell UH-1B Iroquois helicopter
- Bell AH-1E Cobra helicopter
- Curtiss C-46F Commando
- de Havilland YC-7A Caribou
- Douglas VC-47D Skytrain
- Fairchild C-119L Flying Boxcar
- Fairchild C-123K Provider
- Lockheed C-130E Hercules
- Waco CG-15A glider

GOLDSBORO

An F-86 Sabre Jet is on loan from the U.S. Air Force Museum. It entered service in 1955 and was decommissioned in 1970. Originally located in Berkley Memorial Park, it was restored in 1986 and transferred to the police-fire complex in Goldsboro. After another restoration in 2014, it was placed on a pylon at the intersection of West Ash and North Center Streets.

GOLDSBORO

Seymour Johnson AFB

- Canadair CL-13B Sabre Mk. 6
- Fairchild Republic A-10A Thunderbolt II
- McDonnell F-4C Phantom II
- McDonnell F-4E Phantom II
- McDonnell Douglas F-15B Eagle
- North American P-51D-20NA Mustang
- North American F-86E Sabre
- North American F-86H Sabre

- North American F-100A Super Sabre
- Republic F-105D Thunderchief
- Supermarine 329 Spitfire Mk. IIa, replica

HAMLET

DAV Chapter 59, Meeting Location

- Bell UH-1B Iroquois helicopter

HAVELOCK

Marine Corps Air Station Cherry Point

- Consolidated PBY-5A Catalina
- Douglas C-117D Skytrain
- Grumman EA-6A Intruder
- Grumman EA-6A Intruder
- Hawker Siddeley AV-8C Harrier
- Lockheed HC-130B Hercules

JACKSONVILLE

Marine Corps Air Station, New River Aviation Memorial Park

- Bell UH-1N Iroquois helicopter
- Bell AH-1J Sea Cobra helicopter
- Boeing Vertol CH-46E Sea Knight
- McDonnell Douglas F-4C Phantom II
- Piasecki HUP-3 Retriever
- Sikorsky VH-34D Seahorse
- Sikorsky CH-53A Sea Stallion

MIDLAND-BLACK-PHILLIPS

Veterans of Foreign Wars Post 433

A Lockheed T-33A Shooting Star is on display at this Veterans of Foreign Wars (VFW) post. This plane was originally on display at the VFW post in Wilmington. Per the Wilmington VFW page, this plane was flown into Wilmington for an airshow, broke down and was left at the airport.

NEW BERN

Coastal Carolina Regional Airport

- Hawker Siddeley AV-8A Harrier

NEW BERN

Lawson Creek Park

- Grumman F-11F-1 Tiger

NEW SALEM (UNION COUNTY)

Keith Moore American Legion Post 440

- Bell AH-1F Cobra helicopter

NEWTON CONOVER

Veterans of Foreign Wars Post 5305

- Bell UH-1H Iroquois helicopter

SALISBURY

Veterans of Foreign Wars Post 3006

- Bell UH-1H Iroquois helicopter

WAYNESVILLE

Veterans of Foreign Wars Post 5202

- Bell UH-1 Iroquois helicopter

WILMINGTON, NEW HANOVER COUNTY

USS *North Carolina*

- OS2U Kingfisher

This particular Kingfisher crashed on Calvert Island, British Columbia, Canada, in 1946. It was recovered and, in 1970, restored.

APPENDIX A

TUSKEGEE AIRMEN FROM NORTH CAROLINA

There were twenty-five Tuskegee Airmen from the state of North Carolina. The following list gives their names, locations of birth and class numbers/dates. It also lists whether they died during the war.[221]

Second Lieutenant Cecil L. Browder; Wilmington, NC; 43-I-SE, October 1, 1943

Second Lieutenant Fred L. Brower (or Brewer) Jr.; Charlotte, NC; 43-I-SE, October 1, 1943. Died when his plane crashed over the Alps.

Second Lieutenant Willie L. Byrd; Fayetteville, NC; 43-K-TE, December 5, 1943; weather officer, 301st Fighter Squadron

Second Lieutenant Marshall Cabiness; Gastonia, NC; 42-I-SE, October 9, 1942; 301st Fighter Squadron

Second Lieutenant James Y. Carter; Winston-Salem, NC; 43-D-SE, April 29, 1943

Second Lieutenant John H. Chavis; Raleigh, NC; 44-D-SE, April 15, 1944; "Spun into the Adriatic Sea."

Second Lieutenant Conrad H. Cheek; Weldon, NC; 46-C-SE, June 28, 1946 (last class)

Second Lieutenant Quinten V. Cheek; Weldon, NC; 45-F-TE, September 8, 1945

Second Lieutenant Lewis W. Craig; Asheville, NC; 44-D-SE, April 15, 1944

Second Lieutenant Spurgeon N. Ellington; Winston-Salem, NC; 43-E-SE, May 28, 1943; Died in a plane crash near Atlanta on December 10, 1945.

Second Lieutenant Willie H. Fuller; Tarboro, NC; 42-G-SE, August 5, 1942; He was an original member of the Ninety-Ninth Fighter Squadron and an instructor at Tuskegee and completed seventy missions before he returned home.

Second Lieutenant Vernon V. Haywood; Raleigh, NC; 43-D-SE, April 29, 1943; 302nd Fighter Squadron

Second Lieutenant George W. Helm; Reidsville, NC; 45-C-SE, May 23, 1945

Second Lieutenant Aaron Herrington; Raleigh, NC; 44-E-SE, May 23, 1944

Second Lieutenant Andrew J. Johnson; Greensboro, NC; 44-I-SE, November 20, 1944

Second Lieutenant Andrew D. Marshall; Wadesboro, NC; 44-C-SE, March 12, 1944; Went MIA over Greece in December 1944.

Second Lieutenant Harvey L. McClelland; Asheville, NC; 45-A-TE, March 11, 1945

Second Lieutenant Clinton B. Miles; Durham, NC; 45-A-SE, January 14, 1943; He is credited with shooting down a FW190 on February 7, 1944.

Second Lieutenant David J. Murphy Jr.; Whitesville, NC; 44-1-TE, October 16, 1944

Second Lieutenant Francis B. Peoples; Henderson, NC; 44-D-SE, April 15, 1944; Died at Tuskegee on April 27, 1944.

Flight Officer Clarence E. Reynolds; Ahoskie, NC; 45-E-SE, August 4, 1944

Second Lieutenant Robert C. Robinson Jr.; Asheville, NC; 44-G-SE, August 4, 1944; Failed to return from Yugoslavia on June 10, 1944.

Second Lieutenant Graham Smith; Ahoskie, NC; 42-F-SE, July 3, 1942; Ninety-Ninth Fighter Squadron

Flight Officer Reginald V. Smith; Ahoskie, NC; 45-E-SE, August 4, 1945; Ninety-Ninth Fighter Squadron

Second Lieutenant Arthur Wilburn; Asheville, NC; 44-A-SE, January 7, 1944

APPENDIX B

WOMEN'S AIR SERVICE PILOTS (WASP) FROM NORTH CAROLINA

There were twelve Women's Air Service Pilots who were born in North Carolina.[222]

Katherine Lee Harris "Kate" Adams (1919–2002); Durham, Orange County
Ellen Virginia Croxton Ellis (1919–2001); Charlotte, Mecklenburg County
Dorothy Deane Ferguson (1917–1992); Waynesville, Haywood County
Margaret "Peg" Parish Garland (1922–2003); Raleigh, Wake County
Sara Evelyn Payne Hayden (1919–2019); Granite Falls, Caldwell County
Dorothy "Dot" Post Hoover (1917–2015); Buncombe County
Dorothy "Dot" Swain Lewis (1915–2013); near Asheville, Buncombe County
Elizabeth MacKethan Magid (1917–2004); Cumberland County
Mildred Elnora Taylor Marshall (1919–2018); Charlotte, Mecklenburg County
Ethel Gibson Lytch Miller (1921–2000); Raeford, Hoke County
Saran E. Gibson Symmes (1916–2009); Charlotte, Mecklenburg County
Eleanor Elaine Thompson Wortz (1921–2013); Salisbury, Rowan County

APPENDIX C

LOST AIRPORTS

There are scores of lost or abandoned airports from Manteo to Murphy. In the early days of aviation, county fairgrounds, local golf courses and farmers' fields were used as landing locations. Many municipalities outgrew their airfields and then leased or purchased new acreage to accommodate large airplanes. Some of these municipalities used multiple fields at once. The 1945 Sectional Aeronautical Chart, Mecklenburg County, marks five airfields—Cannon, Morris, Delta, Plaza and Brockenbrough—plus an auxiliary field in Huntersville. The following list is just a select few of these landing fields that are no longer in use across the state.

Horace Williams Airport, Chapel Hill

Originally known as Martindale Field and/or Chapel Hill Airport, it started as a grass landing strip in 1923. Purchased by UNC–Chapel Hill in 1940 using Works Progress Administration funds, it was renamed Horace Williams Airport for a professor who gifted additional land to the university. Gerald Ford and George H.W. Bush, along with 18,700 other men, were trained in preflight and reserve officers' programs during World War II. John F. Kennedy visited in October 1961. It was closed by UNC for campus expansion on May 15, 2018.[223]

LOUISBURG AIRPORT/FRANKLIN FIELD, FRANKLIN COUNTY

Discussions about an airport in Louisburg occurred as early as July 1930, when a representative of the U.S. Chamber of Commerce was in town looking to establish a beacon light and emergency landing field for government airplanes carrying mail. The site was west of Louisburg on the property of G.W. Ford, and it appears on the 1938 state highway map. The first airshow in the county was probably held at this site in August 1940. A newspaper in August 1944 stated that a new airport was opened on the "Raleigh highway one mile southwest of town." Yet another site, one mile west of town on the property of J.T. Pruitt, was constructed in 1945. The name of the new airport was Franklin Field. The Louisburg Airport continued to appear in newspaper articles for over a decade, although only Franklin Field appears on maps. Franklin Field continues to appear on sectional charts through 1971. The airport was listed as having an 1,800-foot-long turf runway.[224]

MOUNTAIN WILDERNESS, YANCEY COUNTY

From the mid-1960s to 1977, this was a development that had an airstrip. One advertisement stated residents could "Fly In, Hike In, Camp In." It was destroyed in the flood of 1977.

PEIFFER FIELD, NEW HANOVER COUNTY

Constructed by the Carolina Skyway, this two-runway grass field opened in November 1944. The field was named for naval aviator Carl David Peiffer, the first naval aviator from the Wilmington area to lose his life in World War II. While period newspapers stated the private airfield was located on Wrightsville Beach, it was actually located in Seagate, near Oleander Drive and Peiffer Avenue. Sometimes, Peiffer Field is also referred to as the Carolina Beach Airport. The field was open for approximately five years before it was abandoned.[225]

Skyline Airport, Moore County

First mentioned in 1942 as a forty-three-acre site that was being taken over by the U.S. Army for the purpose of training aviators, Skyline Airport was located near the intersection of U.S. 1 and Young Road, three miles northeast of Southern Pines. The airfield appears on a 1948 topographical map but not on the 1950 map.[226]

Huffman Field/ Fairchild Airport, Burlington

First used as a landing strip in 1919, Hoffman Field opened in 1932, with Lawrence Gwyn opening a flying school there. Two 1,800-foot-long sod runways and several hangars were constructed. The field was purchased by Fairchild Aircraft Company in 1943 and renamed Fairchild Flying Field, also called Fairchild Airport. Toward the end of 1945, there was one 2,500-foot-long paved landing strip. The Fairchild Airport property was auctioned off in June 1967. The airstrip and surrounding property brought in $305,000, all of which was used to enhance the newer Municipal Airport.[227]

Maynard Field, Winston-Salem

Located on Kernersville Road, the landing strip featured intersecting runways, gasoline storage tanks and eventually hangars, a telephone, an on-site mechanic and automobile parking. The field, named for Lieutenant Belvin Maynard, was opened in 1919 and closed sometime in the mid-1930s. A historical marker denotes the site.[228]

Maynard Field in Winston-Salem operated from 1919 until the mid-1930s. This marker was erected in 2008. *Author's collection.*

Halifax County Airport, Roanoke Rapids

The original airport was proposed in October 1944, and the site was inspected in January 1945. In April, the county purchased 280 acres between Roanoke Rapids and Littleton at a cost of $30,000. A year later, the field was graded. The field was leased to the Copenhaver brothers, who offered flying lessons there. The first airshow was held in July 1946, although the airport was not finished until the summer of 1949. A five-person committee was appointed to operate the airport in 1959. The 3,000-foot-long runway was paved in 1961, and new lighting was installed in 1965. The Halifax County airport closed sometime after February 2009, when the Halifax-Northampton Regional Airport opened.[229]

MANTEO AIRPORT/SKYCO FIELD, DARE COUNTY

The first landing field on Roanoke Island was originally called the Manteo Airport. By the 1940s, it bore the name of the community in which it was located: Skyco Airport. The airport appeared in 1938, with Johnny Crowell, "North Carolina's most famous stunt pilot," landing there in January 1939. At the end of that year, when airplanes first participated in the anniversary of the Wright brothers' first flight, they were staged at Manteo Airport. After the construction of the Dare County Airport, the Skyco Airport closed.[230]

ASHEVILLE-HENDERSONVILLE AIRPORT, HENDERSON COUNTY

The Asheville-Hendersonville Airport was in operation from 1928 to 1960. *Buncombe County Special Collections, Pack Memorial Public Library.*

This landing field opened in 1928, a joint venture between the two cities. The airport was often described as the best in western North Carolina. During World War II, the U.S. Army improved the runways. Passenger service after the war included Capital, Delta and Piedmont Airlines. The airport was closed in 1960.

APPENDIX D

EARLY NORTH CAROLINA LANDING FIELDS AND AIRPORTS

1920

- Fayetteville, emergency, large aircraft
- Goldsboro (racetrack), emergency, 150 feet by 750 feet
- Goldsboro, emergency, 150 feet by 600 feet
- Greensboro, emergency
- Hobgood, emergency, 2,400 feet by 1,400 feet
- Hoffman, emergency
- Pinehurst (gold links, racetrack), emergency
- Raleigh, emergency, 4,500 feet by 750 feet
- Weldon, emergency, 750 feet by 150 feet
- Wilmington (country club), emergency, 75 feet by 1,350 feet
- Winston-Salem, emergency, 35 acres[231]

1930

- Asheville, municipal
- Burlington, Williamson Airport, commercial
- Charlotte Airport, commercial
- Chapel Hill, Martindale Field, commercial
- Fayetteville, Pope Field, U.S. Army

- Gastonia, A-NY Airway, intermediate
- Goldsboro Airport, municipal
- Greensboro, Lindely Field, municipal
- Henderson, fairgrounds, auxiliary
- Lexington, A-NY Airway, intermediate
- Minton, A-NY Airway, intermediate
- Monroe, United Field, commercial
- Mooresville, A-NY Airway, intermediate
- New Bern, Acme Field, commercial
- Pinehurst, Knollwood Airport, municipal
- Pinehurst, auxiliary
- Raleigh, Raleigh Airport, commercial
- Raleigh, Marshburn-Robbins Airport, municipal
- Reidsville, A-NY Airway, intermediate
- Reidsville, commercial
- Rockingham, Rockingham Airport, commercial
- Statesville, Statesville Airport, commercial
- Shelby, Shelby Airport, municipal
- Stanly, A-NY Airway, intermediate
- Tarboro, Baker Field, municipal
- Wilmington, Bluethenthal Field, municipal
- Winston-Salem, Miller Airport, municipal[232]

APPENDIX E

1940s NORTH CAROLINA AIR CARRIERS

On September 8, 1947, the *Charlotte Observer* noted that the Civil Aeronautics Board in Washington, D.C., had granted letters of registration to sixty-five North Carolina air transportation companies.

- Alamance Aviation Service, Burlington
- Alvon Air Service, Rocky Mount
- Arrowood Flying Service, Mount Holly
- Bailey's Flying Service, Madison
- Barnes Aircraft, Lumberton
- Best Aviation Company, Raleigh
- Blue Ridge Aviation, Elkin
- Bost's Flying Service, Newton
- Bradford D. Moser, Shelby
- Bridges Aircraft Inc., Shelby
- Bridges Airport, Kings Mountain
- Cannon Aircraft Sales and Service, Charlotte
- Cannon Aviation Company, Hickory
- Carolina Air Park, Concord
- Carolina Aircraft Sales, Charlotte
- Carolina Airways
- Carolina Flying Service, Tarboro
- Carolina Skyways, Wilmington

- Charlotte Flying Service, Charlotte
- Fayetteville Air Service, Fayetteville
- Harold Bachman, Southern Pines
- Harris Aero Service, Mooresville
- Haskell A. Deaton Flying Service, Charlotte
- Henderson Flying Service, Henderson
- Jones Flying Service, Lincolnton
- Lewetta Aviation Service, Concord
- Martin Flying Service, Gastonia
- McCord's Areo Service, Gastonia
- Morrison Aeronca, Kings Mountain
- Mt. Airy Flying Service, Mt. Airy
- New Bern Aviation, New Bern
- Nicholas Flying Service, Black Mountain
- Ocracoke-Manteo Trans. Co., Manteo
- Parker's Airport, Eagle Springs
- Piedmont Aviation, Winston-Salem
- Resort Airlines, Southern Pines
- Rocky Mount Air Service, Rocky Mount
- Salisbury Aircraft Service, Salisbury
- Shelby Flying Service, Shelby
- Skylines, Asheville
- State Airlines, Charlotte
- Tew Aviation Service, Raleigh
- Union Aircraft Corp., Monroe
- United Aero Service, Charlotte
- W&L Airways, Wadesboro
- Warren Brothers Flying Service, Roxboro
- W.B. Glover, Erwin
- Yadkin Valley Flying Service, North Wilkesboro

NOTES

Introduction

1. Aviation Benefits Beyond Borders, "Economic Growth," https://aviationbenefits.org/economic-growth/.

Chapter 1

2. *The North Carolina Gazette*, November 3, 1785; *The North Carolina Gazette*, September 3, 1789; *The North Carolina Star*, November 27, 1828.
3. *North Carolina Constitutional and Peoples' Advocate*, July 9, 1833; *The Raleigh Register*, July 6, 1841; *The Raleigh Register*, June 30, 1846; *Tarboro Press*, June 11, 1845; *Republican and Patriot*, July 10, 1851; *The Daily Journal*, July 5, 1853; Marray, *Wake*, 395; *Asheville Messenger*, April 16, 1851; *Spirit of the Age*, December 12, 1851; *The Semi-Weekly Raleigh Register*, September 25, 1852; *The North Carolina Star*, August 20, 1851; *The Hillsborough Recorder*, June 28, 1854.
4. *Wilmington Journal*, June 5, 1846; *Wilmington Chronicle*, June 10, 1846; *Tri-Weekly Commercial*, November 4, 1846; *Weekly North Carolina Standard*, December 13, 1854.
5. *The Charlotte Journal*, March 28, 1832; *The Greensboro Patriot*, December 10, 1842; *The Democratic Signal*, December 29, 1843; *The Old North State*, September 7, 1850; *The Weekly Star*, May 1, 1891.

6. *The Charlotte Observer*, January 9, 1878; *The Greensboro Patriot*, November 22, 1883; Pleasants, *Home Front*, 53–54.
7. *The Union Republican*, May 30, 1901; *The Union Republican*, November 28, 1901; *The Union Republican*, May 15, 1902; *Winston-Salem Journal*, March 9, 1902; *The Progressive Farmer*, March 4, 1902; *The Progressive Farmer*, July 1, 1902.

Chapter 2

8. Crouch, *Wings*, 47; *Statesville Record and Landmark*, May 15, 1896; *Fisherman and Farmer*, May 15, 1896; *Asheville Daily Citizen*, May 27, 1891.
9. Crouch, *Wings*, 56; McCullough, *Wright Brothers*, 39.
10. Kirk, *First in Flight*, 23; Parramore, *First to Fly*, 65–78.
11. McCullough, *Wright Brothers*, 56–63.
12. McCullough, *Wright Brothers*, 65–81.
13. *Tar Heel*, October 3, 1902; *The Farmer and Mechanic*, October 7, 1902; *The News and Observer*, October 5, 1902; *Minneapolis Journal*, October 8, 1902.
14. McCullough, *Wright Brothers*, 105–7.
15. *The Wilmington Messenger*, December 9, 1903; *The News and Observer*, December 9, 1903.
16. *The Morning Post*, December 23, 1903; *Goldsboro Weekly Argus*, December 24, 1903.
17. *The Wilmington Messenger*, January 7, 1904; *The Charlotte Observer*, January 7, 1904; *The News and Observer*, January 7, 1904; *The Greensboro Patriot*, January 13, 1904; *The Mount Airy News*, January 13, 1904; *Windsor Ledger*, January 14, 1904; *The Asheville News Gazette*, January 6, 1904.
18. Kirk, *First in Flight*, 241, 259, 260.
19. *The News and Observer*, May 2, 1925; *The News and Observer*, March 9, 1929; *The News and Observer*, March 11, 1928; *The News and Observer*, April 6, 1930; *The Chapel Hill News*, February 10, 1933; *The Wilmington Morning Star*, December 18, 1942; National Air and Space Museum, "Original *Wright Flyer*?"
20. Kirk, *First in Flight*, 33, 142, 180.

Chapter 3

21. Parramore, *First to Fly*, 115–23; Liberatore, *Helicopters Before Helicopters*, 74–76.
22. *The Charlotte News*, September 15, 1908; *The Charlotte News*, September 22, 1908; *The Charlotte News*, October 20, 1908; *The Charlotte News*, October 23, 1908; *The Salisbury Post*, October 7, 1908; *The Greensboro Record*, October 15, 1908.
23. *The Weekly Standard*, July 28, 1858; *The Tarborough Southerner*, August 7, 1858; *The Greensboro Patriot*, October 12, 1888; *The Goldsboro Headlight*, October 4, 1888; *The Daily Journal*, February 18, 1900; *King's Weekly*, April 13, 1900; *The Asheville Times*, June 10, 1900; *The Asheville Times*, September 21, 1900; *The Robesonian*, August 3, 1900; *The News and Observer*, September 6, 1900; *The Charlotte News*, September 19, 1900; *The News Reporter*, September 21, 1900; *The News Reporter*, October 5, 1900; *The North Wilkesboro Hustler*, September 28, 1900; *Winston-Salem Journal*, October 2, 1900; *The Roanoke News*, October 4, 1900; *The Roanoke News*, November 8, 1900; *Henderson Gold Leaf*, October 4, 1900; *Henderson Gold Leaf*, November 8, 1900; *The Franklin Times*, October 5, 1900; *The Morning Post*, October 5, 1900.
24. *The Daily Free Press*, October 2, 1900; *The Wilmington Messenger*, August 10, 1889; *The Raleigh Times*, April 16, 1908; *The News and Observer*, August 26, 1908; Ritter, "Pack Man," 2.
25. Parramore, *First to Fly*, 130–31, 135; *The Wilmington Dispatch*, August 25, 1909; *The Wilmington Morning Star*, June 16, 1910; *The Wilmington Morning Star*, June 21, 1910; *The Wilmington Morning Star*, November 15, 1910.
26. *The Gastonia Gazette*, September 9, 1910; *The Caucasian*, October 6, 1910; *The Raleigh Times*, June 25, 1910; *The Raleigh Times*, October 25, 1910; *The News and Observer*, September 24, 1910.
27. *The Charlotte News*, November 11, 1910; *The Charlotte News*, November 13, 1910; *The News and Observer*, November 5, 1910; *The News and Observer*, November 17, 1910; *The Herald Sun*, December 4, 1910; *Winston-Salem Journal*, December 1, 1911.
28. *The Wilmington Morning Star*, March 12, 1911; *The Wilmington Morning Star*, April 30, 1911; *The Wilmington Dispatch*, April 3, 1911; *The News and Observer*, April 9, 1911; *The News and Observer*, May 4, 1911; *The News and Observer*, October 17, 1911; *High Point Enterprise*, November 3, 1911; *The Dispatch*, November 8, 1911.

29. *The Gastonia Gazette*, May 14, 1912; *The Gastonia Gazette*, June 13, 1913; *The Gastonia Gazette*, September 28, 1915; *The Wilmington Morning Star*, July 5, 1913; *The Chronicle*, June 11, 1914; *The Daily Journal*, April 28, 1914; *The Daily Journal*, May 29, 1914; *The News and Observer*, October 18, 1914; *Oxford Public Ledger*, September 25, 1915.
30. *The Wilmington Morning Star*, January 16, 1915; *The Wilmington Morning Star*, February 17, 1915; *The Wilmington Dispatch*, January 22, 1915; *The Wilmington Dispatch*, February 4, 1915; *The News and Observer*, February 2, 1915; *The Charlotte Observer*, July 12, 1915; *The Charlotte Observer*, July 14, 1915; *The Charlotte Observer*, July 15, 1915; *The Charlotte Observer*, July 17, 1915; Parramore, *First to Fly*, 187–90.
31. *The Charlotte Observer*, February 13, 1917; *Public Laws and Resolutions*, 139.
32. Crouch, *Wings*, 151.
33. Mullally, "First American Aerial Victory," 27–34.
34. Hall and Nordhoff, *Lafayette Flying Corps*, 1:115, 342–44, 407–10.
35. Lemmon and Midgette, *Carolina and the Two World Wars*, 71; *The Charlotte News*, June 2, 1918; *The Charlotte News*, June 13, 1918; *The Charlotte News*, June 27, 1918; *The Charlotte Observer*, June 17, 1918.
36. Parramore, *First to Fly*, 238–39.
37. *Oxford Public Ledger*, May 15, 1918; *The Charlotte Observer*, July 14, 1918; *Rockingham Post-Dispatch*, August 1, 1918; Bandel, *North Carolina and the Great War*, 37.

Chapter 4

38. *Asheville Citizen-Times*, April 18, 1919; *Asheville Citizen-Times*, June 12, 1919; *Asheville Citizen-Times*, June 20, 1919; *Asheville Citizen-Times*, June 21, 1919; *Asheville Citizen-Times*, August 13, 1919; *Asheville Citizen-Times*, August 19, 1919; *The News and Observer*, April 26, 1919; *Hickory Daily Record*, July 9, 1919.
39. *The Gastonia Gazette*, December 27, 1918; *The Wilmington Morning Star*, April 25, 1919; *The Wilmington Morning Star*, May 2, 1919; *The Wilmington Morning Star*, June 2, 1919; *The Wilmington Morning Star*, July 27, 1919; *The Messenger and Intelligencer*, May 8, 1919; *The Messenger and Intelligencer*, July 3, 1919; *The Chatham Record*, May 22, 1919; *The News and Observer*, June 18, 1919; *Rockingham Post-Dispatch*, July 19, 1919; *Salisbury Evening Post*, August 8, 1919.
40. *The News and Observer*, April 16, 1919.

41. *The News and Observer*, May 29, 1919; *The News and Observer*, June 13, 1919; *The News and Observer*, June 15, 1919; *The News and Observer*, June 17, 1919; *The News and Observer*, July 8, 1919; *Greenville News*, May 31, 1919; *The Messenger and Intelligencer*, June 19, 1919; *Rockingham Post-Dispatch*, July 17, 1919; *Salisbury Evening Post*, June 25, 1919; *Salisbury Evening Post*, June 28, 1919.
42. *Salisbury Evening Post*, November 4, 1919; *Salisbury Evening Post*, November 7, 1919; *The News and Observer*, December 6, 1919; *The Charlotte News*, September 9, 1922.
43. *The Wilmington Morning Star*, January 2, 1912; *The News and Observer*, May 17, 1918.
44. *Statesville Record and Landmark*, May 26, 1916; *The Pinehurst Outlook*, March 3, 1920; *The Gastonia Gazette*, January 15, 1920; *The News and Observer*, December 21, 1918; *The News and Observer*, June 2, 1920; *The News and Observer*, July 27, 1920; *The News and Observer*, October 6, 1920; *The News and Observer*, September 18, 1925; Powell, *Through Four Centuries*, 477; Crouch, *Wings*, 221; Allaz, *History of Air Cargo*, 63.
45. Crouch, *Wings*, 235.
46. *The Gastonia Gazette*, November 25, 1919; see also, Crouch, *Wings*, 219.
47. *The Greensboro Record*, September 15, 1923; *The Greensboro Record*, December 1, 1924; *The Greensboro Record*, July 19, 1925; *The Greensboro Record*, June 23, 1925; *News and Record*, September 19, 1923; *News and Record*, May 30, 1925; *News and Record*, June 16, 1925; Arnett, *Greensboro*, 156–57.
48. *The Charlotte Daily Observer*, May 21, 1910; *The Charlotte Daily Observer*, April 16, 1919; *The Charlotte News*, October 31, 1910; *The Charlotte News*, July 21, 1919; *The Charlotte News*, March 25, 1920; *The Charlotte News*, February 25, 1921; *The Charlotte News*, July 15, 1929.
49. *The Charlotte Observer*, October 21, 1919; *The Charlotte Observer*, October 25, 1919; *The Charlotte Observer*, October 29, 1919.
50. *The Charlotte News*, May 2, 1920; *The Charlotte News*, May 16, 1920.
51. *The Charlotte News*, May 26, 1920; *The Charlotte Observer*, June 3, 1920; *The Charlotte Observer*, December 14, 1920; *The Charlotte Observer*, February 14, 1921; *The Charlotte Observer*, February 1, 1924; *The Charlotte Observer*, November 24, 1925; *The Charlotte Observer*, March 19, 1927.
52. *The Charlotte Observer*, August 8, 1926; *The Charlotte Observer*, October 29, 1926; *The Charlotte Observer*, October 30, 1926; *The Charlotte Observer*, January 12, 1927; *The Charlotte Observer*, January 26, 1927; *The Charlotte News*, July 17, 1927.

53. *The Charlotte News*, April 9, 1928; *The Charlotte News*, April 16, 1928; *The Charlotte News*, June 4, 1928; *The Charlotte News*, June 20, 1928; *The Charlotte Observer*, October 21, 1928; *The Charlotte Observer*, November 11, 1928; *The Charlotte Observer*, November 12, 1928; *The Charlotte Observer*, November 29, 1928; *The Charlotte Observer*, April 1, 1930.
54. *The News and Observer*, April 9, 1911; *The Wilmington Dispatch*, January 1, 1912; *The Sentinel*, March 14, 1912; *The Sentinel*, June 5, 1919; *The Sentinel*, June 13, 1919; *The Sentinel*, July 2, 1919; *The Sentinel*, July 11, 1919; *The Sentinel*, October 23, 1919; Fries, Wright and Hendricks, *Forsyth*, 253; Turner, "Quest to Build," 289–95.
55. *Asheville Citizen-Times*, July 5, 1921; *Asheville Citizen-Times*, March 26, 1950; *The News and Observer*, August 10, 1913; *The News and Observer*, April 4, 1920; *The Asheville Times*, May 9, 1920; *The Asheville Times*, January 9, 1921; *The Asheville Times*, August 28, 1930.
56. *Asheville Citizen-Times*, February 3, 1927; *Asheville Citizen-Times*, August 20, 1928; *Asheville Citizen-Times*, August 23, 1928; *Asheville Citizen-Times*, August 27, 1928; *Asheville Citizen-Times*, August 22, 1936; *Asheville Citizen-Times*, September 26, 1936; *Asheville Citizen-Times*, December 10, 1936; *Asheville Citizen-Times*, July 17, 1937; *Asheville Citizen-Times*, October 5, 1937; Buncombe County Special Collections, "Landing Strips."
57. *The News and Observer*, December 21, 1918; *The News and Observer*, January 2, 1919; *The News and Observer*, January 18, 1919; *The News and Observer*, May 29, 1919; *The News and Observer*, October 26, 1919; *The News and Observer*, November 1, 1919; *The News and Observer*, March 31, 1920; *The News and Observer*, April 1, 1920.
58. *The News and Observer*, January 9, 1924; *The News and Observer*, September 2, 1926; *The News and Observer*, November 19, 1926; *The News and Observer*, July 7, 1927; *The News and Observer*, July 8, 1927; *The News and Observer*, July 24, 1927; *The News and Observer*, August 10, 1927; *The News and Observer*, January 15, 1928.
59. *The News and Observer*, March 22, 1928; *The News and Observer*, April 30, 1928; *The News and Observer*, June 11, 1928; *The News and Observer*, June 23, 1928; *The News and Observer*, July 14, 1928; *The News and Observer*, September 30, 1929.
60. *The News and Observer*, April 20, 1929; *The News and Observer*, April 24, 1929; *The News and Observer*, May 2, 1929; *The News and Observer*, September 20, 1929.
61. *The News and Observer*, November 6, 1931; *The News and Observer*, September 10, 1934; *Asheville Citizen-Times*, October 5, 1934.

62. *Fayetteville Weekly Observer*, May 28, 1919; *The Wilmington Morning Star*, June 10, 1919; *The Wilmington Morning Star*, August 4, 1919.
63. *The Wilmington Morning Star*, May 26, 1920; *The Wilmington Morning Star*, April 16, 1922; *The Wilmington Morning Star*, May 4, 1922; *The Wilmington Morning Star*, August 26, 1922; *The News and Observer*, February 6, 1928; *The News and Observer*, October 26, 1928.
64. *The News and Observer*, November 19, 1926; *The News and Observer*, October 15, 1927; *The News and Observer*, November 6, 1931; *The News and Observer*, October 5, 1934; *The Caswell Messenger*, October 20, 1927; *The Sandhill Citizen*, November 13, 1931; *The Pilot*, January 17, 1930; *The Pilot*, November 13, 1931.
65. *News and Record*, October 24, 1919; *News and Record*, October 19, 1923; *News and Record*, April 6, 1925; *The News and Observer*, August 31, 1928; *The News and Observer*, June 20, 1930; *Hoke County Journal*, December 6, 1928; *The Moore County News*, May 29, 1930; *The Daily Press*, February 17, 1937.
66. *Asheville Citizen-Times*, October 18, 1934; *Asheville Citizen-Times*, October 28, 1934; *The Charlotte Observer*, October 19, 1934.
67. "Chapter 63: Aeronautics," in *General Statutes of North Carolina*, 11:27–30.
68. *The News and Observer*, May 30, 1921; *The News and Observer*, November 29, 1929; *Dare County Times*, February 3, 1939; *The Seashore News*, June 22, 1939.
69. *Stanly News and Press*, June 6, 1924; *Stanly News and Press*, October 24, 1930; *The News and Observer*, July 6, 1927; *The News and Observer*, November 29, 1927; *The Asheville Times*, May 25, 1930; *The Pilot*, June 31, 1936; *Watauga Democrat*, June 11, 1931; *The Messenger and Intelligencer*, December 3, 1923.
70. *The News and Observer*, December 17, 1919; *The News and Observer*, June 7, 1929; *The Albemarle Press*, June 13, 1929.
71. *The News and Observer*, April 27, 1925; *The News and Observer*, June 16, 1925; *The Sandhill Citizen*, June 28, 1925.
72. *The News and Observer*, May 30, 1925; *The News and Observer*, September 23, 1928; *The Pilot*, March 22, 1929; *The Asheville Times*, June 19, 1935.
73. *The News and Observer*, January 9, 1924; *The Pilot*, February 11, 1938; *Stanly News and Press*, June 27, 1939.
74. Maurer, *Aviation in the U.S. Army*, 118–20, 127; *The News and Observer*, September 6, 1923; *New York Times*, September 7, 1925.
75. Maurer, *Aviation in the U.S. Army*, 224–26; *Stanly News and Press*, December 20, 1927.

76. *The Charlotte News*, October 18, 1931; *The Charlotte News*, October 28, 1931; *The Charlotte Observer*, March 16, 1932; *The Greensboro Record*, December 8, 1930; *The Pilot*, December 18, 1931.
77. *Winston-Salem Journal*, December 6, 1933; *Hickory Daily Record*, December 21, 1933; *The Charlotte News*, December 14, 1933; *Statesville Daily Record*, December 15, 1933; *The Herald Sun*, December 23, 1933; *The Salisbury Post*, December 20, 1933; *The News and Observer*, December 23, 1933.
78. *News and Record*, January 3, 1934; *The Charlotte Observer*, January 7, 1934; *The Charlotte Observer*, January 9, 1934; *Stanly News and Press*, February 21, 1939.
79. *The News and Observer*, July 21, 1929; *The News and Observer*, September 19, 1929; *The News and Observer*, November 1, 1929.
80. *Stanly News and Press*, July 8, 1930; *The News and Observer*, July 4, 1930; *The News and Observer*, November 24, 1931; *The Cleveland Star*, August 13, 1930; *Asheville Citizen-Times*, August 28, 1930; *Asheville Citizen-Times*, September 2, 1930; *Asheville Citizen-Times*, November 25, 1931; *The Chatham Record*, September 10, 1931; *The Charlotte Observer*, November 22, 1931; *Winston-Salem Journal*, November 23, 1931; *News and Record*, November 24, 1931; *The Salisbury Post*, November 25, 1931.
81. *The Elkin Tribune*, March 24, 1932; *The Cleveland Star*, April 28, 1933; *The Cleveland Star*, May 12, 1933; *The Cleveland Star*, October 27, 1933; *The Asheville Times*, February 9, 1930; *The Asheville Times*, August 10, 1935; *The Durham Sun*, November 13, 1933; *The Chapel Hill News*, November 17, 1933; *The Journal Patriot*, May 6, 1935; *The News and Observer*, April 6, 1937.
82. Bigger, *World War II*, 193; Strickland, *The Putt-Putt Air Force*, iii.
83. *Asheville Citizen-Times*, October 13, 1920; *Asheville Citizen-Times*, June 14, 1940; *News and Record*, June 22, 1940; *The Pilot*, June 21, 1940; *The Pilot*, August 23, 1940; Strickland, *The Putt-Putt Air Force*, 43, 108.
84. Strickland, *The Putt-Putt Air Force*, 4; *The Pilot*, June 21, 1940; *The News and Observer*, April 24, 1981.
85. Dew, *Queen City at War*, 53–62.

Chapter 5

86. Best, *Carolina's Shining Hour*, 18.
87. *The Asheville Times*, December 10, 1941; *Gastonia Gazette*, December 9, 1941; *Gastonia Gazette*, December 30, 1941; *Gastonia Gazette*, March 3, 1942; *The Wilmington Morning Star*, January 14, 1942; *Asheville Citizen*,

February 12, 1942; J.M. Horner Jr., letter to C.C. McGinnis, February 20, 1942, box 1, World War II Papers.

88. Hickam, *Torpedo Junction*, 11; O'Neal, *Ocracoke Island*, 23; Bunch, *U-Boats off the Outer Banks*, 183; Gannon, *Operation Drumbeat*, xviii; Keefer, *From Maine to Mexico*, 392.
89. Blazich, "North Carolina's Flying Volunteers," 408, 419.
90. Keefer, *From Maine to Mexico*, 387, 391–92.
91. Blazich, "North Carolina's Flying Volunteers," 420.
92. Warner and Grove, *Base Twenty-One*, 54–55.
93. Warner and Grove, *Base Twenty-One*, 58, 61, 63, 73.
94. Warner and Grove, *Base Twenty-One*, 63–64, 80.
95. Bunch, *U-Boats off the Outer Banks*, 167, 175–77.
96. Blazich, "North Carolina's Flying Volunteers," 328.
97. Pleasants, *Home Front*, 137; *The News and Observer*, January 15, 1942; *Gastonia Gazette*, May 13, 1942; *The Pilot*, May 29, 1942; *The Wilmington Morning Star*, February 24, 1943; N.C. Greene, letter to George K. Snow, March 28, 1943, box 24, World War II Papers; Van A. Covington, letter to gentlemen, April 1, 1943, box 24, World War II Papers; P. Bruce Bateman, letter to Ben E. Douglas, box 40, September 1, 1942, World War II Papers; Colonel William S. Pritchard, letter to Roy I. McMillan, February 17, 1943, box 48, World War II Papers.
98. *The Salisbury Post*, July 4, 1941.
99. J. Allan Dunn, letter to General W.H. Frank, April 28, 1941, box 1, World War II Papers; Lottie Hood, letter to General Walter H. Frank, box 23, July 1, 1941, World War II Papers; W.F. Nufer, letter to Third Interceptor Command, February 5, 1942, box 23, World War II Papers; *Winston-Salem Journal*, May 25, 1942.
100. *The Charlotte News*, June 4, 1942; *The Wilmington Morning Star*, June 19, 1942; *The Wilmington Morning Star*, October 31, 1942; *The Wilmington Morning Star*, March 14, 1943; *The News and Observer*, July 27, 1942; *The News and Observer*, July 31, 1942; *Hickory Daily Record*, June 6, 1942.
101. Lieutenant James F. Garger Jr., letter to Colonel J.W. Harrelson, December 20, 1941, box 23, World War II Papers.
102. *The Wilmington Morning Star*, July 27, 1942; *The Wilmington Morning Star*, February 28, 1943; *The Robesonian*, July 29, 1943; *The News and Observer*, January 11, 1943; *The Herald Sun*, April 28, 1943; *Rocky Mount Telegram*, May 13, 1943.
103. *Fort Bragg at War*, 12; Buchanan, *Soaring Life's Currents*, 91; Mitchell, *From the Pilot Factory*, 102–3.

104. *The Goldsboro Herald*, August 1, 1940; *The Goldsboro Herald*, August 23, 1940; *The Goldsboro Herald*, October 17, 1940; *News and Record*, January 4, 1941; Sroda, *Falling Down for the Count*, 62–63.
105. Wilder and Wilder, *Two Came Thru*, 74–77.
106. Stevens and McCallum, *Camp Mackall*, 31–32, 93.
107. "46th Bomb Group Welcomed to Morris Field," *Morris Code*, November 17, 1943, 3; Rutter, *Wreaking Havoc*, 44, 46, 53; Pleasants, *Home Front*, 86–87.
108. *Wilmington Star News*, November 14, 2021.
109. Tyndall, *Greetings*, 53–55, 59.
110. Tyndall, *Greetings*, 93–94.
111. Landdeck, *Women with Silver Wings*, 160–70; Stallman, *Women in the Wild Blue*, 93, 96, 220; Tyndall, *Greetings*, 93–94.
112. Davis, *North Carolina in World War II*, 47–50.
113. *The News and Observer*, September 5, 1920; *The Pilot*, August 23, 1940; *The Greensboro Record*, November 29, 1932; Pleasants, *Home Front*, 89–90; *The Times*, December 6, 1970; *The Charlotte Observer*, June 9, 1943; *The Asheville Times*, September 23, 1943.
114. Rains, "Raleigh-Durham Army Air Field," 943; Okerstrom, *Project 9*, 108; *The News and Observer*, April 25, 1993; *The Shelby Daily Star*, October 13, 1945.
115. *Asheville Citizen*, October 3, 1940; *Asheville Citizen*, October 13, 1940; *Asheville Citizen*, November 28, 1943; *The Charlotte Observer*, April 22, 1942.
116. *Asheville Citizen-Times*, August 11, 1943; Morgan, *Man Who Flew the* Memphis Belle, 239–42.
117. Eller, *Piedmont Airlines*, 24; *The Sentinel*, June 26, 1942; Elliott, *Piedmont*, 213.
118. Pleasants, *Home Front*, 84; Stoesen, *Guilford County*, 51, 53.
119. Willoughby, *Coast Guard in World War II*, 38, 40.
120. Pleasants, *Home Front*, 56.
121. Davis, *North Carolina in World War II*, 90–91; Bryce, *Liaison Pilot*, 18.
122. Dorr, *Marine Air*, 55.
123. Thole, *Forgotten Fields*, 1:152.
124. *The Chowan Herald*, February 1, 1945.
125. Pleasants, *Home Front*, 195–200.
126. Pleasants, *Home Front*, 103, 107; *Stanly News and Press*, October 8, 1940; *Asheville Citizen-Times*, January 19, 2017; *Dare County Times*, May 21, 1943.

127. *News and Record*, April 25, 1944; Cornell Law School, "*United States v. Causby et ux.*"
128. Strickland, *The Putt-Putt Air Force*, 13; Francis, *Tuskegee Airmen*, 41.
129. Reavis, interview.

Chapter 6

130. *The News and Observer*, November 8, 1948.
131. *The News and Observer*, June 24, 1946; *The Charlotte Observer*, October 28, 1946.
132. *Hickory Daily Record*, January 1, 1940; *Hickory Daily Record*, July 1, 1942; *Hickory Daily Record*, June 23, 1944; *Hickory Daily Record*, April 29, 1946; *The Sentinel*, September 15, 1944; *The Sentinel*, January 3, 1948; *The Wilmington Morning Star*, October 31, 1947; *Winston-Salem Journal*, October 8, 1949.
133. Eller, *Piedmont Airlines*, 20, 23, 33, 48; Elliott, *Piedmont*, 69.
134. Elliott, *Piedmont*, 73, 77, 91, 94, 109.
135. Elliott, *Piedmont*, 115, 118.
136. Elliott, *Piedmont*, 124, 144, 151.
137. Elliott, *Piedmont*, 163, 169, 177, 187, 197.
138. Wadelington, "Wheeler Airlines," 22–24.
139. *The News and Observer*, February 12, 2000.
140. "Charlotte Quartermaster Depot/Charlotte Area Missile Plant."
141. Winkler, *Searching the Skies*, 114.
142. *Civil Defense*, 7; *The Greensboro Record*, June 17, 1972; *The News and Observer*, August 10, 2008; *The Charlotte Observer*, April 17, 2023.
143. *The Durham Sun*, August 10, 1950; *The Charlotte Observer*, April 25, 1952; *The Charlotte Observer*, May 22, 1953; *The Charlotte News*, September 18, 1952; *The Greensboro Record*, October 16, 1952; *Asheville Citizen-Times*, May 13, 1953; *Asheville Citizen-Times*, June 13, 1953; *Mount Olive Tribune*, January 1, 1954; *The News of Orange County*, February 18, 1954; Biddix and Hollifield, *Spruce Pine*, 118.
144. *The Charlotte Observer*, February 4, 1953; *The Durham Sun*, May 23, 1953; *Asheville Citizen-Times*, May 27, 1953; Altieri, "Minutemen and Roentgens," 43–50.
145. *The News of Orange County*, February 2, 1961.
146. *The Wilmington Messenger*, January 12, 1907; *News and Record*, September 12, 1956; *News and Record*, July 19, 1957; *The Reidsville Review*,

May 20, 1957; *The Charlotte News*, July 12, 1957; *The News and Observer*, September 21, 1957; *The Charlotte Observer*, October 6, 1957; *Winston-Salem Journal*, October 81, 1957.

147. Trippe quote in Petzinger, *Hard Landings*, 17.
148. Fly, "What's Past Is Prologue."
149. Fly Fayetteville Regional Airport, "History."
150. Piedmont Triad International Airport, "History."
151. Wilmington International Airport, "History and Future."
152. Raleigh-Durham International Airport, "History."
153. City of Charlotte, "Aviation."
154. Division of Aviation, North Carolina Department of Transportation, "State of Aviation"; *The News and Observer*, June 17, 2024.

Chapter 7

155. *The Charlotte Observer*, June 12, 1932.
156. *The Wilmington Dispatch*, November 24, 1913.
157. Tucker, "Rockwell," 5:242.
158. Parramore, *First to Fly*, 252–69.
159. *The News and Observer*, August 29, 1908; *Hickory Daily Record*, March 4, 1964.
160. *The Charlotte News*, October 17, 1983.
161. Bower, *North Carolina Aviatrix*,
162. Yerkey, *A Pilot's Pilot*,
163. *The News and Observer*, February 2, 1921; *The News and Observer*, February 11, 1932; *The News and Observer*, April 24, 1981; *The Reidsville Review*, January 10, 1950.
164. *Times Union*, March 17, 1929; *Winston-Salem Journal*, April 10, 1938; *The Greensboro Record*, August 27, 1948.
165. *News and Record*, July 19, 1997.
166. *Rocky Mount Telegram*, August 22, 1969.
167. Wegner, "Nicholson."
168. U.S. Air Force, "Spivey."
169. *Asheville Citizen-Times*, September 20, 1976.
170. *The Charlotte Observer*, September 21, 1950; *The Charlotte Observer*, April 5, 1985; *The Charlotte Observer*, April 6, 1985.
171. *The Charlotte Observer*, July 7, 1932.

172. *The Fresno Bee*, November 10, 2013.
173. *Asheville Citizen-Times*, March 31, 2015.
174. Hatch, *Changing Our World*, 145.
175. *The Salisbury Post*, March 17, 2000.
176. *News and Record*, April 23, 1999.
177. Morgan, *Man Who Flew the* Memphis Belle,
178. CAF RISE ABOVE Squadron, "Adams."
179. *The Miami Herald*, January 4, 1995.
180. Howell, "Extraordinary Life."
181. *The News and Observer*, May 4, 2003.
182. *Hickory Daily Record*, July 5, 2014.
183. Lundquist, *Len*, 357; *The Charlotte Observer*, January 26, 1989.
184. *The Robesonian*, May 29, 2010.
185. *News and Record*, April 21, 1957; *News and Record*, April 22, 1957.
186. Pugh Funeral Home, "McGlohon Obituary."
187. Haynsworth and Toomey, *Amelia Earhart's Daughters*, 217; *The Telegraph*, January 2, 2020.
188. Duggins, *Final Countdown*, 44–46.
189. Gubert, Sawyer and Fannin, *Distinguished African Americans*, 35.
190. Duke and Duke, *Moon Walker*,
191. Guttman, "Only Ace Pilot."
192. Wadelington, "Wheeler Airlines,"
193. Summer, "Tar Heels in Space," 26.
194. Summer, "Tar Heels in Space," 27.
195. Summer, "Tar Heels in Space," 28.
196. Summer, "Tar Heels in Space," 26.
197. Summer, "Tar Heels in Space," 26.
198. *Pensacola News Journal*, March 4, 2001; *Florida Today*, May 7, 2011.
199. *The Charlotte Observer*, January 17, 2013.
200. *Florida Today*, April 25, 2022; NASA, "Bob Hines."

Chapter 8

201. Aviation Safety Network, "Boeing B-17."
202. *The Virginia-Pilot*, April 2, 1943.
203. Blake, *River of Cliffs*, 212.
204. *The Charlotte Observer*, June 9, 1943.

205. Stevens and MacCallum, *Camp Mackall*, 95.
206. Bureau of Aircraft Accidents Archives, "Crash of a Martin PBM-3D Mariner."
207. *The Salisbury Post*, September 25, 1944.
208. *The Charlotte Observer*, June 15, 1944.
209. *Asheville Citizen-Times*, September 20, 2010.
210. *Statesville Daily Record*, October 7, 1949.
211. *The Daily Tar Heel*, November 18, 1953.
212. *The Charlotte News*, January 6, 1960.
213. *Hickory Daily Record*, July 19, 1967.
214. *Statesville Record and Landmark*, March 9, 1973.
215. *The Charlotte Observer*, September 12, 1974.
216. *The Charlotte Observer*, February 21, 1988.
217. *Asheville Citizen-Times*, Marsh 25, 1994.
218. *The Charlotte Observer*, July 3, 1994.
219. *Statesville Record and Landmark*, December 15, 1994.
220. *The Charlotte Observer*, January 9, 2003.

Appendix A

221. Francis, *Tuskegee Airmen*, 277; Tuskegee University, "Pilot Listing."

Appendix B

222. Texas Woman's University, "Training Classes."

Appendix C

223. Vickers, *Chapel Hill*, 143; *The Chapel Hill Herald*, October 22, 2000.
224. *The Franklin Times*, July 25, 1930; *The Franklin Times*, August 9, 1940; *The Franklin Times*, August 4, 1944; *The News and Observer*, June 7, 1945.
225. *The Wilmington Morning Star,* December 1, 1944; December 6, 1944, July 22, 1945; *Wilmington Star News,* May 11, 1947.
226. *The Pilot*, July 3, 1942; *The Pilot*, April 16, 1943.
227. *The Daily Times-News*, November 30, 1932; *The Daily Times-News*, June 9, 1967; *The Durham Sun*, May 22, 1943; *The Herald Sun*, April 19, 1968.

228. Forsyth Historic Resources Commission, "Historical Marker."
229. *Roanoke Rapids Daily Herald*, November 2, 1944; *Roanoke Rapids Daily Herald*, January 4, 1945; *Roanoke Rapids Daily Herald*, April 5, 1946; *Roanoke Rapids Daily Herald*, May 16, 1946; *The Virginia-Pilot*, March 22, 1946; *Rocky Mount Telegram*, January 19, 1949; *Rocky Mount Telegram*, January 18, 1965; *The Herald Sun*, October 7, 1959; *The Herald Sun*, July 28, 1961.
230. *Ledger Star*, January 10, 1939; *Asheville Citizen-Times*, December 16, 1939.

Appendix D

231. *Aircraft Year Book*, 322.
232. *The Charlotte Observer*, November 22, 1930.

BIBLIOGRAPHY

Newspapers

The Albemarle Press
Asheville Citizen
Asheville Citizen-Times
Asheville Daily Citizen
Asheville Messenger
The Asheville News Gazette
The Asheville Times
The Caswell Messenger
The Caucasian
The Chapel Hill Herald
The Chapel Hill News
The Charlotte Daily Observer
The Charlotte Journal
The Charlotte News
The Charlotte Observer
The Chatham Record
The Chowan Herald
The Chronicle
The Cleveland Star
The Daily Free Press
The Daily Journal
The Daily Press
The Daily Tar Heel
The Daily Times-News
Dare County Times
The Democratic Signal
The Dispatch
The Durham Sun
The Elkin Tribune
The Farmer and Mechanic
Fayetteville Weekly Observer
Fisherman and Farmer
Florida Today
The Franklin Times
The Fresno Bee
The Gastonia Gazette
The Goldsboro Headlight
The Goldsboro Herald
Goldsboro Weekly Argus
The Greensboro Patriot
The Greensboro Record
Greenville News
Henderson Gold Leaf
The Herald Sun

Hickory Daily Record
High Point Enterprise
The Hillsborough Recorder
Hoke County Journal
The Journal Patriot
King's Weekly
Ledger Star
The Messenger and Intelligencer
The Miami Herald
Minneapolis Journal
The Moore County News
The Morning Post
The Mount Airy News
Mount Olive Tribune
The News and Observer
News and Record
The News of Orange County
The News Reporter
New York Times
North Carolina Constitutional and Peoples' Advocate
The North Carolina Gazette
The North Carolina Star
The North Wilkesboro Hustler
The Old North State
Oxford Public Ledger
Pensacola News Journal
The Pilot
The Pinehurst Outlook
The Progressive Farmer
The Raleigh Register
The Raleigh Times
The Reidsville Review
Republican and Patriot
The Roanoke News
Roanoke Rapids Daily Herald
The Robesonian
Rockingham Post-Dispatch
Rocky Mount Telegram
Salisbury Evening Post
The Salisbury Post
The Sandhill Citizen
The Seashore News
The Semi-Weekly Raleigh Register
The Sentinel
The Shelby Daily Star
Spirit of the Age
Stanly News and Press
Statesville Daily Record
Statesville Record and Landmark
Tarboro Press
The Tarborough Southerner
Tar Heel
The Telegraph
The Times
Times Union
Tri-Weekly Commercial
The Union Republican
The Virginia-Pilot
Watauga Democrat
Weekly North Carolina Standard
The Weekly Standard
The Weekly Star
Wilmington Chronicle
The Wilmington Dispatch
Wilmington Journal
The Wilmington Messenger
The Wilmington Morning Star
Wilmington Star News
Windsor Ledger
Winston-Salem Journal

Archives

Reavis, Virginia. Oral interview. September 17, 2000. Women Veterans Historical Project. University of North Carolina–Greensboro. Greensboro, NC.

World War II Papers, Office of Civilian Defense. North Carolina Division of Archives and History. Raleigh, NC.

Articles

Altieri, Jayson A. "Minutemen and Roentgens: A History of Civil Air Patrol's Aerial Radiological Monitoring Program." *Air Power History* 68, no. 1 (Spring 2021): 43–51.

Blazich, Frank A., Jr. "North Carolina's Flying Volunteers: The Civil Air Patrol in World War II, 1941–1945." *North Carolina Historical Review* 89, no. 4 (October 2012): 399–442.

"46th Bomb Group Welcomed to Morris Field," *Morris Code*, (November 17, 1943): 3

Mullally, Erin. "First American Aerial Victory." *Aviation History*, May 2008.

Rains, Rusty. "Raleigh-Durham Army Air Field." In *Encyclopedia of North Carolina.* Edited by William S. Powell. The University of North Carolina Press, 2006.

Summer, Jim. "Tar Heels in Space." *Tar Heel Junior Historian* 43, no. 1 (Fall 2003): 26–29.

Tucker, Glenn. "Kiffin Yates Rockwell." In *Dictionary of North Carolina Biography.* 6 vols. University of North Carolina Press, 1994.

Turner, Walter R. "The Quest to Build a Great Airport in Winston-Salem." *American Aviation Historical Society* 41 (2006): 288–95.

Wadelington, Charles W. "Wheeler Airlines." *Tar Heel Junior Historian* 43, no. 1 (Fall 2003): 22–24.

Books

Aircraft Year Book. Manufacturers Aircraft Association Inc., 1920.

Allaz, Camille. *The History of Air Cargo and Airmail.* Christopher Foyle, 2005.

Arnett, Ethel S. *Greensboro, North Carolina.* The University of North Carolina Press, 1955.

Bandel, Jessica A. *North Carolina and the Great War, 1914–1918.* North Carolina Office of Archives and History, 2017.

Best, Mary, ed. *North Carolina's Shining Hour.* Our State Books, 2005.

Biddix, David, and Chris Hollifield. *Spruce Pine.* Arcadia Publishing, 2009.

Bigger, Margaret G., ed. *World War II: Hometown and Home Front Heroes.* A. Borough Books, 2003.

Blake, Christopher. *River of Cliffs: A Linville Gorge History.* The History Press, 2017.

Bower, Jennifer B. *North Carolina Aviatrix Viola Gentry: The Flying Cashier.* The History Press, 2015.

Bryce, James R. *Liaison Pilot.* Sunflower University Press, 2002.

Buchanan, Jean P. *Soaring Life's Currents: The Memoir of Charles O. Gordon, Sr.* Branden House Publishing, 2003.

Bunch, Jim. *U-Boats off the Outer Banks: Shadow in the Moonlight.* The History Press, 2017.

Charlotte-Mecklenburg Landmark Commission. "Charlotte Quartermaster Depot/Charlotte Area Missile Plant." 2021.

Civil Defense in North Carolina. The North Carolina Council of Civil Defense, 1956.

Crouch, Tom D. *Wings: A History of Aviation from Kites to the Space Age.* W.W. Norton & Company, 2004.

Davis, Anita Price. *North Carolina in World War II: A Documentary Portrait.* McFarland and Company Inc., 2015.

Dew, Stephen H. *The Queen City at War: Charlotte, North Carolina During World War II, 1939–1945.* University Press of America, 2001.

Dorr, Robert F. *Marine Air: The History of the Flying Leathernecks in Words and Photos.* Berkley, 2005.

Duggins, Pat. *Final Countdown: NASA and the End of the Space Shuttle Program.* University Press of Florida, 2009.

Duke, Charles, and Dotty Duke. *Moonwalker: The True Story of an Astronaut Who Found that the Moon Wasn't High Enough to Satisfy His Desire for Success.* Oliver-Nelson Books, 1990.

Eller, Richard E. *Piedmont Airlines: A Complete History, 1948–1989.* McFarland and Company Inc., 2008.

Elliott, Frank. *Piedmont: Flight of the Pacemaker.* Piedmont Aviation Historical Society, 2006.

Fort Bragg at War: The Station Complement. U.S. Army, 1945.

Francis, Charles E. *The Tuskegee Airmen: The Men who Changed a Nation.* Braden Books, 2008.

Fries, Adelaide, Stuart Thompson Wright and J. Edwin Hendricks. *Forsyth: The History of a County on the March.* The University of North Carolina Press, 1976.

Gannon, Michael V. *Operation Drumbeat: The Dramatic True Story of Germany's First U-Boat Attacks Along the American Coast in World War II.* Naval Institute Press, 2009.

The General Statutes of North Carolina: Annotated. Vol. 11. The Mitchell Company, 1990.

Gubert, Betty Kaplan, Miriam Sawyer and Carolina M. Fannin. *Distinguished African Americans in Aviation and Science.* Oryx Press, 2002.

Hall, James N., and Charles Bernard Nordhoff, eds. *The Lafayette Flying Corps.* 2 vols. Houghton Mifflin Harcourt Company, 1920.

Hatch, Sybil E. *Changing Our World: True Stories of Women Engineers.* American Society of Civil Engineers, 2006.

Haynsworth, Leslie, and David Toomey. *Amelia Earhart's Daughters: The Wild and Glorious Story of American Women Aviators from World War II to the Dawn of the Space Age.* William Morrow & Company, 1998.

Hickam, Homer. *Torpedo Junction: U-Boat War off America's East Coast, 1942.* New York: Naval Institute Press, 1996.

Keefer, Louis E. *From Maine to Mexico with America's Private Pilots in the Fight Against Nazi U-Boats.* COTU Publishing, 1997.

Kirk, Stephen. *First in Flight: The Wright Brothers in North Carolina.* John F. Blair, 1995.

Landdeck, Katherine Sharp. *The Women with Silver Wings.* Crown, 2021.

Lemmon, Sarah, and Nancy Midgette. *North Carolina and the Two World Wars.* North Carolina Office of Archives and History, 2013.

Liberatore, E.K. *Helicopters Before Helicopters.* Krieger Publishing Company, 1998.

Lundquist, Wayne. *Len the Pilot.* Xlibris, 2011.

Marray, Elizabeth Reid. *Wake, Capital County of North Carolina.* Volume 1. Capital County Publishing, 1983.

Maurer, Maurer. *Aviation in the U.S. Army, 1919–1939.* Office of Air Force History, 1987.

McCullough, David. *The Wright Brothers.* Simon and Schuster, 2015.

Mitchell, William P. *From the Pilot Factory, 1942.* Texas A&M University Press, 2005.

Morgan, Robert. *The Man Who Flew the* Memphis Belle. Dutton, 2001.

Okerstrom, Dennis R. *Project 9: The Birth of the Air Commandos in World War II.* University of Missouri Press, 2014.

O'Neal, Earl W. *Ocracoke Island: Its People, the U.S. Coast Guard & Navy Base During World War II.* Self-published, 2001.

Parramore, Thomas C. *First to Fly: North Carolina and the Beginnings of Aviation.* The University of North Carolina Press, 2002.

Petzinger, Thomas, Jr. *Hard Landing: The Epic Contest for Power and Profits That Plunged the Airlines into Chaos.* Three Rivers Press, 1996.

Pleasants, Julian M. *Home Front: North Carolina During World War II.* University Press of Florida, 2017.

Powell, William S. *North Carolina Through Four Centuries.* The University of North Carolina Press, 1989.

Public Laws and Resolutions of the State of North Carolina Passed by the General Assembly at Its Session of 1917. Edwards & Broughton, 1917.

Rutter, Joseph W. *Wrecking Havoc: A Year in an A-20.* Texas A&M Press, 2004.

Sroda, Becky. *Falling Down for the Count: The Letters and Diaries of Albert Williams from 1943–1945.* Trafford, 2003.

Stallman, David A. *Women in the Wild Blue: Target-Towing WASP at Camp Davis.* Self-published, 2006.

Stevens, Lowell, and Tom McCallum. *Camp Mackall and Its Times in the Sandhills of North Carolina.* Richmond County Historical Society, 2011.

Stoesen, Alexander R. *Guilford County: A Brief History.* North Carolina Division of Archives and History, 1993.

Strickland, Patricia. *The Putt-Putt Air Force: The Story of the Civilian Pilot Training Program and the War Training Service (1934–1944).* Department of Transportation, 1971.

Thole, Lou. *Forgotten Fields of America: World War II Bases and Training, Then and Now.* Vol. 1. Pictorial Histories Publishing, 1996.

Tyndall, Clifford. *Greetings from Camp Davis.* Chapel Hill Press Inc., 2006.

Vickers, James. *Chapel Hill: An Illustrated History.* Barclay Publishers, 1985.

Warner, Melvin J., and George W. Grove. *Coastal Patrol Base Twenty-One.* N.p., 1944.

Wilder, Burton, and Jean Wilder. *Two Came Thru.* Vantage Press, 1998.

Willoughby, Malcom F. *The U.S. Coast Guard in World War II.* U.S. Naval Institute, 1957.

Winkler, David F. *Searching the Skies: The Legacy of the United States Cold War Defense Radar Program.* Air Combat Command, 1997.

Yerkey, Gary G. *A Pilot's Pilot: Gen. Caleb V. Haynes and the Rise of American Air Power, 1917–1944.* Createspace, 2018.

Online

Aviation Benefits Beyond Borders, "Economic Growth," https://aviationbenefits.org/economic-growth.

Aviation Safety Network. "Boeing B-17 Flying Fortress." https://aviation-safety.net/wikibase/97285.

Buncombe County Special Collections. "Asheville's Landing Strips." https://specialcollections.buncombecounty.org/2014/07/27/ashevilles-landing-strips/.

Bureau of Aircraft Accidents Archives. "Crash of a Martin PBM-3D Mariner Flying Boat in Hertford: 9 Killed." https://www.baaa-acro.com/crash/crash-martin-pbm-3d-mariner-flying-boat-hertford-9-killed.

CAF RISE ABOVE Squadron. "Kate Lee Harris Adams." https://cafriseabove.org/kate-lee-harris-adams/.

City of Charlotte. "Aviation." http://charlottenc.gov/City-Government/Departments/Aviation.

Cornell Law School. "*United States v. Causby et ux.*" https://www.law.cornell.edu/supremecourt/text/328/256.

Division of Aviation, North Carolina Department of Transportation. "North Carolina: The State of Aviation." https://www.ncdot.gov/divisions/aviation/Documents/state-of-aviation.pdf.

Fly. "What's Past Is Prologue: Making History…Again." https://www.fly.com/article/whats-past-prologue-making-history-again.

Fly Fayetteville Regional Airport. "History." https://www.flyfay.com/about-us/history.

Forsyth Historic Resources Commission. "Historical Marker Program." https://www.cityofws.org/DocumentCenter/View/4042/15---Maynard-Field-PDF.

Guttman, Jon. "The Air Force's Only Ace Pilot." The History Net. https://www.historynet.com/air-force-only-ace-pilot-vietnam-war/.

Howell, Ross, Jr. "The Extraordinary Life of WWII Flying Ace George E. Preddy, Jr." *O'Henry Magazine*, December 2019. https://ohenrymag.com/an-ordinary-american-boy.

NASA. "Bob Hines, NASA Astronaut." https://www.nasa.gov/people/bob-hines/.

National Air and Space Museum. "What Happened to the Original *Wright Flyer*?" https://airandspace.si.edu/stories/editorial/what-happened-original-wright-flyer.

Piedmont Triad International Airport. "Airport History." https://flyfrompti.com/airport-history/.

Pugh Funeral Home. "John Anderson McGlohon Obituary." https://www.pughfuneralhome.com/obituaries/john-mcglohon.

Raleigh-Durham International Airport. "RDU History." https://www.rdu.com/airport-authority/history/.

Ritter, Lisa. "Pac Man: Charles Broadwick Invented a New Way of Falling." *Air and Space Magazine* 25, no. 1 (May 2010): 68–72. https://www.smithsonianmag.com/air-space-magazine/pack-man-10601089/.

Texas Woman's University. "Training Classes." https://twu.edu/library/womans-collection/collections/women-airforce-service-pilots-official-archive/research/training-classes/.

Tuskegee University. "Tuskegee Airmen Pilot Listing." https://www.tuskegee.edu/support-tu/tuskegee-airmen/tuskegee-airmen-pilot-listing.

U.S. Air Force. "Major General Delmar Taft Spivey." https://www.af.mil/About-Us/Biographies/Display/Article/105568/major-general-delmar-taft-spivey/.

Wegner, Ansley. "Nicholson, Mary." NCPedia. https://www.ncpedia.org/nicholson-mary.

Wilmington International Airport. "History and Future of ILM." http://flyilm.com/airport-history/.

INDEX

A

Albemarle, North Carolina 60, 62
Asheboro, North Carolina 141, 152
Asheville, North Carolina 9, 12, 17, 23, 26, 29, 35, 39, 44, 45, 47, 48, 55, 56, 57, 59, 62, 63, 64, 66, 67, 81, 93, 94, 107, 108, 112, 114, 115, 118, 126, 132, 133, 134, 136, 149, 165, 166, 167, 172, 173, 176

B

Beachey, Lincoln 6, 23, 26, 27, 39, 46, 47, 53
Beaufort County, North Carolina 30
Beaufort, North Carolina 71, 72, 73, 74, 144
Bickett, Thomas 36, 38, 39
Blowing Rock, North Carolina 74, 76
Bluethenthal, Arthur 30, 53, 125
Broadwick, Tiny 6, 24
Buncombe County, North Carolina 56, 115, 118, 134, 167
Burke County, North Carolina 7, 118, 148
Burlington, North Carolina 62, 100, 105, 117, 171, 173, 175
Buxton, North Carolina 59

C

Camel City Flying Service 47, 107, 136
Camp Davis, North Carolina 84, 85, 87, 93
Camp Greene, North Carolina 31, 43, 44, 45
Camp Lejeune, North Carolina 77
Camp Mackall, North Carolina 80, 159

Camp Polk, North Carolina 31, 49
Cape Hatteras, North Carolina 60, 69, 71, 72, 79, 147
Capital Airlines 120, 121
Carolina Beach, North Carolina 53, 170
Carteret County, North Carolina 22, 90
Carthage, North Carolina 30, 153, 160
Cary, North Carolina 117
Castle Hayne, North Carolina 24
Catawba County, North Carolina 139
Chapel Hill, North Carolina 9, 19, 57, 64, 67, 99, 112, 116, 117, 130, 143, 144, 169, 173
Charlotte, North Carolina 6, 9, 10, 17, 23, 25, 28, 31, 33, 37, 39, 40, 43, 44, 45, 46, 55, 56, 58, 59, 60, 61, 62, 63, 64, 67, 70, 76, 81, 82, 105, 108, 110, 111, 112, 113, 115, 117, 118, 122, 125, 128, 133, 139, 142, 145, 150, 151, 154, 160, 165, 167, 173, 175, 176
Chatham County, North Carolina 31, 114, 150
Cherry Point, North Carolina 90, 104, 114, 156, 162
Cherry, R. Gregg 108
Cherryville, North Carolina 64
Clayton, North Carolina 125, 141
Clinton, North Carolina 38, 160, 166
Columbus County, North Carolina 142
Concord, North Carolina 35, 36, 37, 43, 44, 175, 176
Crinkly, Andrew 67
Cumberland County, North Carolina 78, 167
Currituck County, North Carolina 98

D

Davis, Tom 6, 107, 108, 139
Doolittle, Jimmy 6
Duke, Charlie 6
Dunn, North Carolina 131
Durham, North Carolina 25, 26, 37, 38, 51, 61, 64, 92, 110, 111, 112, 115, 121, 122, 136, 137, 143, 150, 166, 167

E

Earhart, Amelia 6, 18, 51, 54, 129, 131, 134, 157
Eden, North Carolina 140
Edenton, North Carolina 12, 98
Ehringhaus, John 51
Elizabeth City, North Carolina 13, 14, 19, 96, 110, 160
Elizabethtown, North Carolina 145
Elkin, North Carolina 64, 175

F

Fayetteville, North Carolina 31, 36, 55, 67, 118, 145, 146, 154, 161, 165, 173, 176
Fort Bragg, North Carolina 31, 36, 41, 77, 78, 80, 103, 149, 150, 161
Fort Caswell, North Carolina 53

Fort Fisher, North Carolina 85, 114, 155
Franklin, North Carolina 23, 130, 170
Fuquay-Varina, North Carolina 134

G

Gardner, Max 38
Gastonia, North Carolina 28, 39, 41, 74, 107, 165, 174, 176
Gatesville, North Carolina 132
Gatling, James H. 10
Goldsboro, North Carolina 9, 17, 25, 26, 37, 41, 63, 64, 79, 80, 116, 161, 173, 174
Granite Falls, North Carolina 167
Granville County, North Carolina 23
Greensboro, North Carolina 9, 10, 17, 23, 26, 28, 35, 37, 40, 41, 42, 43, 46, 54, 61, 95, 101, 110, 111, 117, 120, 131, 132, 136, 138, 151, 166, 173, 174
Greenville, North Carolina 23, 37, 90, 112, 134, 151
Guilford County, North Carolina 42, 115, 140

H

Halifax County, North Carolina 56, 172
Hamlet, North Carolina 37, 80, 162
Harnett County, North Carolina 130
Havelock, North Carolina 155, 162
Henderson, North Carolina 174, 176
Hendersonville, North Carolina 48, 55, 56, 57, 59, 62, 64, 66, 67, 93, 94, 118, 149, 156, 172
Hertford County, North Carolina 10, 102
Hickory, North Carolina 6, 35, 72, 105, 106, 118, 123, 157, 175
High Point, North Carolina 26, 34, 37, 42, 46, 56, 67, 95, 101, 120
Hillsboro, North Carolina 115
Hoffman, North Carolina 80, 171, 173
Huntersville, North Carolina 62, 133, 169
Hyde County, North Carolina 57

J

Johnston County, North Carolina 125

K

Kill Devil Hills, North Carolina 13, 15, 19, 20, 112, 157, 158
Kinston, North Carolina 23, 37, 72, 90, 108, 112
Kitty Hawk, North Carolina 5, 12, 13, 14, 15, 16, 17, 18, 19, 20, 54, 147

L

Langley, Samuel P. 10, 12, 16, 17
Laurinburg, North Carolina 59, 80, 92, 98, 144, 147, 148

Lexington, North Carolina 54, 108, 126, 174
Lincolnton, North Carolina 36, 37, 176
Lindbergh, Charles 6, 45, 54, 95, 107, 118, 130
Littleton, North Carolina 23, 171
Louisburg, North Carolina 37, 130, 170
Lumberton, North Carolina 23, 28, 36, 63, 77, 102, 175

M

Madison, North Carolina 107, 175
Manteo, North Carolina 70, 71, 73, 97, 158, 169, 172, 176
Martin County, North Carolina 131
Maxton, North Carolina 67, 81, 92, 98, 147, 148
Maynard, Belvin 6, 31, 38, 43, 46, 48, 126, 127, 171
McDowell County, North Carolina 7, 56, 149
Mebane, North Carolina 43, 62, 100
Mocksville, North Carolina 134, 136
Mooresville, North Carolina 37, 174, 176
Morehead City, North Carolina 33, 107
Morgan, Robert 6, 93, 136
Morganton, North Carolina 24, 35, 127
Morrison, Cameron 38
Mt. Airy, North Carolina 17, 176
Mt. Holly, North Carolina 23, 107
Mt. Olive, North Carolina 58, 115

N

Nash County, North Carolina 58
New Bern, North Carolina 23, 28, 36, 49, 98, 104, 108, 112, 163, 174, 176
New Hanover County, North Carolina 28, 83, 121, 149, 164, 170
North Wilkesboro, North Carolina 23, 176

O

Ocracoke Island, North Carolina 69
Onslow County, North Carolina 84, 90, 102
Orange County, North Carolina 132, 133, 167

P

Piedmont Airlines 6, 107, 110, 111, 112, 118, 120, 121, 136, 139, 143, 149, 152, 158, 172
Pinehurst, North Carolina 26, 39, 41, 44, 58, 97, 118, 144, 173, 174
Post, Wiley 6, 63, 130
Preddy, George, Jr. 6, 138, 152

R

Raeford, North Carolina 167
Raleigh, North Carolina 6, 9, 15, 17, 19, 23, 25, 26, 28, 31, 36,

37, 38, 39, 45, 49, 50, 51, 54, 55, 57, 59, 60, 62, 65, 66, 67, 74, 76, 77, 92, 104, 110, 111, 112, 114, 121, 122, 127, 130, 131, 134, 138, 140, 141, 150, 151, 165, 166, 167, 170, 173, 174, 175, 176
Randolph County, North Carolina 140, 141
Reidsville, North Carolina 40, 143, 166, 174
Reynolds, Zachary Smith 46, 47, 50, 94, 107, 133
Rickenbacker, Eddie 6, 51, 54, 76
Roanoke Island, North Carolina 57, 172
Robeson County, North Carolina 139, 140
Rockingham, North Carolina 31, 36, 37, 58, 80, 129, 140, 174
Rockwell, Kiffin 29, 30, 126
Rocky Mount, North Carolina 36, 175, 176
Rowan County, North Carolina 31, 167
Rutherford County, North Carolina 56

S

Salisbury, North Carolina 9, 23, 26, 37, 54, 56, 61, 63, 76, 123, 164, 167, 176
Sanford, North Carolina 58, 112, 141
Scotland Neck, North Carolina 58
Selma, North Carolina 68, 141
Shelby, North Carolina 28, 62, 64, 174, 175, 176
Shinn, Conrad 6, 140
Southern Pines, North Carolina 55, 74, 108, 110, 171, 176
Spencer, North Carolina 158
Stanly County, North Carolina 57
Statesville, North Carolina 9, 12, 24, 25, 36, 45, 61, 127, 133, 145, 174
Stokes County, North Carolina 10, 11
Surry County, North Carolina 129

T

Tarboro, North Carolina 9, 37, 59, 107, 137, 138, 166, 174, 175

U

Union County, North Carolina 128, 129, 163

V

Vance County, North Carolina 127, 128

W

Wadesboro, North Carolina 36, 37, 58, 166, 176
Warren County, North Carolina 23
Watauga County, North Carolina 58
Waynesville, North Carolina 164, 167
Weaverville, North Carolina 25

Weldon, North Carolina 23, 165, 173
Westall, Henry 35, 36, 43, 48
Wheeler Airlines 111, 144
Wheeler, Warren 6, 111, 143
Williamsboro, North Carolina 39
Wilmington 9, 17, 19, 24, 26, 28, 30, 31, 38, 41, 53, 61, 62, 67, 71, 74, 76, 77, 83, 85, 100, 107, 108, 116, 121, 125, 163, 164, 165, 170, 173, 174, 175
Wilson County, North Carolina 31
Wilson, North Carolina 31, 33, 112
Windsor, North Carolina 17
Winston-Salem, North Carolina 10, 23, 26, 35, 38, 42, 45, 46, 54, 55, 57, 61, 63, 67, 94, 104, 107, 108, 111, 113, 114, 120, 133, 136, 165, 166, 171, 173, 174, 176
Wright, Orville 5, 12, 13, 14, 15, 16, 17, 18, 19, 20, 22, 29, 130, 157, 158
Wrightsville Beach, North Carolina 47, 53, 62, 170
Wright, Wilbur 5, 12, 13, 14, 16, 17, 18, 19, 20, 29, 157

Y

Yancey County, North Carolina 170
Youngsville, North Carolina 23

ABOUT THE AUTHOR

Michael C. Hardy has a passion for North Carolina history. Among his twenty-six published books are a history of the Toe River Valley, studies of Confederate regiments like the Thirty-Seventh North Carolina and Fifty-Eighth North Carolina Troops and a pictorial history of Grandfather Mountain. His ancestors lived in Surry and Wilkes Counties, marching with Colonel Benjamin Cleveland to fight at the Battle of Kings Mountain during the Revolutionary War. In 2010, Michael was named the Historian of the Year by the North Carolina Society of Historians. When not researching, writing or lecturing, Michael spends his time volunteering at historical sites as an interpreter.